THE EUROPEAN LIBRARY
EDITED BY J. E. SPINGARN

THE FAILURE

[Un Uomo Finito]

By
GIOVANNI PAPINI
Author of "Life of Christ"

Authorized translation by
VIRGINIA POPE

New York
Harcourt, Brace and Company

PRINTED IN THE U. S. A. BY

THE QUINN & BODEN COMPANY

RAHWAY, N. J

Tu non se' morta, ma se' ismarrita
Anima nostra, che sì ti lamenti.
DANTE.

(O soul of mine so piteously lamenting,
Thou art not dead but only stunned awhile.)

Contents

Andante

Appassionato

Tempestoso

CONTENTS

Solenne

Lentissimo

Allegretto

"All his life he lived alone and wild."
ARIOSTO.

Chapter 1: A Torn Photograph

I WAS never a child; I never had a childhood.

I cannot count among my memories warm, golden days of childish intoxication, long joyous hours of innocence, or the thrill of discovering the universe anew each day. I learned of such things later on in life from books. Now I guess at their presence in the children I see. I was more than twenty when I first experienced something similar in myself, in chance moments of abandonment, when I was at peace with the world. Childhood is love; childhood is gaiety; childhood knows no cares. But I always remember myself, in the years that have gone by, as lonely, sad, and thoughtful.

Ever since I was a little boy I have felt tremendously alone—and "peculiar."

I don't know why.

It may have been because my family was poor or because I was not born the way other children are born; I cannot tell. I remember only that when I was six or seven years old a young aunt of mine called me *vecchio*—"old man," and the nickname was adopted by all my family. Most of the time I wore a long, frowning face. I talked very little, even with other children; compliments bored me; baby-talk

3

angered me. Instead of the noisy play of the companions of my boyhood I preferred the solitude
of the most secluded corners of our dark, cramped,
poverty-stricken home. I was, in short, what ladies
in hats and fur coats call a "bashful" or a "stubborn"
child; and what our women with bare heads and
shawls, with more directness, call a *rospo*—a "toad."

They were right.

I must have been, and I was, utterly unattractive
to everybody. I remember, too, that I was well aware
of the antipathy I aroused. It made me more "bashful," more "stubborn," more of a "toad" than ever.
I did not care to join in the games played by other
boys, but preferred to stand apart, watching them
with jealous eyes, judging them, hating them. It
wasn't envy I felt at such times: it was contempt;
it was scorn. My warfare with men had begun even
then and even there. I avoided people, and they
neglected me. I did not love them, and they hated
me. At play in the parks some of the boys would
chase me; others would laugh at me and call me
names. At school they pulled my curls or told the
teachers tales about me. Even on my grandfather's
farm in the country peasant brats threw stones at me
without provocation, as if they felt instinctively that
I belonged to some other breed. My relations, when
they visited us, never called me to them, never petted
me, except when the merest sense of decency seemed
to demand it. I sensed the insincerity of such caresses
and hid myself away in silence; when I was forced

to answer their questions I was rude, discourteous, and impudent.

One memory is engraved on my heart more deeply than any other: chill, damp, Sunday evenings of November or December spent at my grandfather's; a steaming bowl of punch in the middle of the table; a great bronze oil lamp hanging from the rafters; roasted chestnuts in a deep bowl passing from hand to hand; and all around the board the flushed faces of our numerous family—aunts, uncles, cousins, in greater numbers than I could count.

The patriarch, white and keen of wit, would sit by the fireside laughing and drinking. Under a light covering of ash the embers would crackle; the glasses would clink as they hit the plates; my aunts, bigoted, small-minded creatures, oozing with the scandal and the gossip of the week, would raise their voices in hideous chatter, as their offspring scrambled about the floor piercing the blue clouds of paternal smoke with shrieks and laughter. The noise of this stupid, miserly party made my soul and my head ache. I felt a stranger in that gathering—worlds apart from all of them. As soon as I could, unnoticed, I would slip out of the room, and feeling my way along a damp wall, come to the long dark passage leading to the outer entrance. My poor, lonely, little heart would beat as if I were about to commit a crime. A glass door opened from the passageway upon a small uncovered court. Pushing it gently ajar, I would stand listening to the rain as it dripped from the roof upon the pavement or into the puddles under the eaves—a tired, listless, reluctant drip falling without enthusiasm, without decision, with that steady lifelessness, with that stupid galling obstinacy, of things that never end. I would listen to it there in the dark, the cool air fanning my face, my eyelids wet with raindrops; and if some capricious flurry splashed my cheek I was as happy as if it had come to purify me, to invite me out with it into the clean distances—far from houses, far from Sunday evening family parties. But soon a voice would call me back to light, to misery, to a chorus of reproaches: "Where did that boy get his manners?"

Yes, it is true, I never was a child. I was an "old man," "a toad," thoughtful and sullen.

Even from those early days the best of my life was within me. Cut off from joy and affection I withdrew into my inner self as a wild animal into its den, hiding myself away, stretching my cramped limbs, gaping with a bloodthirsty hunger which I satisfied with raw and eager dreams, in a lonely introspection into my empty soul, a fierce contemplation of the world as I saw it through that empty soul. Such was my only refuge, such my only joy. No one "liked" me. Hatred imprisoned me in solitude. Solitude made me sadder and more unlikeable; unhappiness stupefied my heart but stimulated my mind. I was "peculiar"—I was "different." My "difference" separated me from those nearest me, and with the widening breach my "peculiarity" increased. At the very outset of life I began to taste, if not to understand, the sweetness, which only grown men for the most part feel, of that infinite and indefinable melancholy which spurns tears and groans and consolations, and which, content wtih its very lack of purpose, feeds on itself, little by little forming the habit of a selfish, secluded, wholly inward life, learning not to depend on others, separating itself forever from its fellow-men.

No, I have never known what it was to be young, nor can I recall having been a child. I was shy and pensive always, retiring and silent always, without a smile, without a single outburst of spontaneous joy.

I recognize myself in the pale and bewildered creature my first picture shows.

The photograph is small, dirty, faded, and torn through the middle just under the heart; the edges of the pasteboard mounting around it are black, like bands of mourning. The washed-out face of a dreamy child is turned toward the left—because in that direction, as you feel, there happens to be no one whose gaze he must endure. The eyes are sad and a little sunken (perhaps the photograph was not a good one!); the mouth is firmly closed, its lips pressed one upon the other as if to hide the teeth. One feature of beauty only: long soft curls that lie in a tangled mass on a sailor collar.

My mother says I was seven when this photograph was taken. Perhaps I was. I have no other proof of my childhood. But could you call this the picture of a child—the weazened, bleached, misshapen ghost, that does not look at me, that refuses to look at anybody?

It is not hard to see that these eyes were never intended to reflect the blue of the skies—they are gray and cloudy, by nature. These cheeks that are white and pale—they will always be white and pale. No blush will ever come to them (except from fatigue or from shame). And these lips, so tightly, so wilfully, closed were never made to be parted in a smile, nor were they made for speech, for prayer, for shouts of glee. They are the lips of a man who will suffer pain, but never betray it with a cry. They are lips that will be kissed too late in life.

In this bit of faded photograph I find the dead soul of those early days of mine; the sickly face of a "toad," the frown of a "sullen," a "stubborn" child, the self-possessed dejection of an "old man." I feel a grip at my heart as I think of all those dreary days, of all those endless years, of that fettered, imprisoned life, of that purposeless useless anguish, of that insatiable homesick longing for other skies and other comrades.

No, no, this is not the picture of a child. I must insist again: I never had a childhood.

Chapter 2: A Hundred Books

A MAD craving for knowledge rescued me from my solitude. Ever since I solved the mysteries of my speller, line by line, letter by letter—fat, squatty letters, lower-case, but in broad-faced type; impeccably moral illustrations in wood-cut; and winter evenings (how cold they were, how far away they seem!) as I sat under the big lamp, the lamp shade painted with blue flowers and yellow, beside my mother, still young, alone there save for me, her black hair shining in the lamp-light as she bent over her sewing—I have had no greater pleasure, no surer solace, than reading. My clearest and most cherished recollections of those years are not of my first blue velvet sailor cap; nor of oranges sucked dry at the edge of a stagnant garden pool; nor of stately tin war-horses vainly prancing on their strips of wood; nor yet of a first mysterious tingling felt in the presence of a little girl, panting, her lips half-opened, after a run at my side. Instead, I recall, with a still childish longing, my first or second reader, a poor, humble, wretchedly stupid book bound in light yellow pasteboard—on the cover a model boy, plump and pious, kneeling beside a narrow iron bed, and apparently saying the rhymed prayer I could spell out below. And my homesick yearning is even greater when I remember a kind of

9

"Arabian Nights" of nature, a monstrous tome in a frayed green binding, its vast pages crumpled and rusty with dampness, many of them torn half in two or soiled with thumb marks and ink spots, which I always opened with the certainty of finding a marvel that was ever new though I had seen it many times before. There gigantic devil-fish with great, round, cruel eyes rose from the Pacific Ocean to catch big sailing vessels in their embrace; a tall youth knelt (his hat on, however) on the top of a mountain, casting a colossal shadow out against a murky German sky; between the steep towering cliffs of a Spanish mountain gorge rode a diminutive knight, his armor barely gilded with a ray of light from the sky so far above—frightened, he seemed, by the silence of that awful abyss; a sleepy Chinese god—with nothing on but a piece of cloth hanging from his waist, a hammer in one hand and a chisel in the other—was putting the finishing touches on the World, chipping off the points of stiff, brittle stalagmites that rose in a jumbled forest from the earth about him; on the edge of a promontory, facing a white, stormy Polar Sea, stood a daring explorer, buried in his furs, unfurling a black wind-tattered flag to Arctic gales. Turning a reddened page or two, I would come upon fantastic skeletons of prehistoric monsters; dumb faces of Polynesian savages; coral islands floating like skiffs on a tropical sea; terrifying comets hurtling with long yellow tails across limitless ink-black skies that shrank in horror before them.

Among the first books to fall into my hands was a badly dilapidated copy of the memoirs of Garibaldi. I read and reread it, not understanding, yet instinctively stirred by all that smell of powder, all that flashing of sabers, all that spectacle of red-shirted outlaws riding to victory. I had not a trace of definite information in my head. I did not know what Italy was nor what a war was; but I had to give vent to my excitement somehow, so I made a sketch of the General's bearded face on the fly-leaf of the book; and that seemed to make him something alive and close to me.

One of the supreme moments of my life was when my father gave me full privileges over the family library, which was a round wicker basket—containing a hundred books or more—forgotten in a small storeroom in our rear attic, high up under the gables and overlooking the roofs of the houses around. That room became the veritable Alhambra of my dreams. All sorts of odds and ends had accumulated there—fire-wood, cast-off rags, mouse-traps, bird cages, a National Guard musket and a red, moth-eaten Garibaldi shirt (on it a medal of the '60 campaign).

Every day, the instant I was free, I locked myself up in that room, and, one by one, handling them with awe and almost fearful circumspection, drew the discarded books from their hiding place, poor dilapidated things, their covers gone, their backs broken, Volume II's without Volume I's, pages missing, or torn or crumpled, spotted with fly-specks or pigeon dung—

but so rich and glorious in surprises, wonders, and promises for me. I read here and there; I deciphered; I did not always understand; if I grew tired, I would begin afresh, so impatient was the ecstasy I felt at these my first approaches to the worlds of poetry, adventure, or history, which a word, a phrase, a picture, would evoke for a fleeting instant before my eyes.

I did not stop at reading: I dreamed; I meditated; I reconstructed; struggling to divine the meaning of it all. Those books were sacred things in my eyes. I believed every word they said. I was unable to distinguish between history and legend, between fact and fancy; printed letters stood for infallible truth to me.

My reality was not the life I knew at home, in school, on the streets, but the world of those books, where I felt myself most alive. On scorching afternoons in summer I was with Garibaldi galloping across the pampas of Uruguay with herds of cattle, bullets showering around him, his cape blowing in the wind; damp rainy mornings I spent with Count Alfieri coursing behind spans of horses and miles of verses along all the post-roads of Europe; my nights were nights of patriotic hatreds or of oratorical frenzies of glory, passed in company with the illustrious men whose acquaintance I made in Plutarch's "Lives,"—dozens of tiny volumes, I remember, bound in blue paper and printed in very small type.

Moreover, those books gave me my first impulse to think. Down toward the bottom of that marvelous basket I found five or six large green volumes (a col-

lection of aphorisms of Voltaire compiled by some
infidel) in which God and Theology were overthrown
and the Bible and the priests of the Church held up
to ridicule. Among the many other things in that first
hundred books was a copy also of Carducci's "Hymn
to Satan"; and from the day I found that poem I
have always felt a greater love for the Rebellious
Angel under the earth than for the majestic Old Fogey
who dwelt in the heavens. Later on I came to realize
how crude and unsound all that anti-religious apolo-
getic was; but to it I owe the fact, be it good or bad,
that I am a man for whom *God has never existed*.
Born of a father who was an atheist, baptized without
his knowledge by my mother, brought up in ignorance
of church and catechism, I have never had a so-called
"crisis of the soul," a "night of Jouffroy," a "discovery
of the death of God." For me God never died because He never lived in my heart.

There was another book which had a great influence
on my mind at that time and consequently during later
years: "The Praise of Folly," by Erasmus of Rotter-
dam. We had an Italian translation of that book in
the house, illustrated with the sharp and spirited wood-
cuts of Holbein. I read and reread it several times
with indescribable delight. Perhaps to Erasmus I
owe my passion for unusual thoughts and my profound conviction that when men are not fools they
are scoundrels.

Chapter 3: A Million Books

AFTER a few years of voracious and disordered reading I found that the limited number of books we had at home (plus those I borrowed from the scant collections of friends and relatives, plus second-hand volumes which I bought with the few pennies I would steal from my mother or save from my allowances for recess) were hopelessly insufficient. An older boy told me of rich and magnificent libraries in town which were open to everybody and where any book could be had for the asking—best of all, without spending a cent.

I decided to go there at once.

There was however one difficulty: to gain admission to those paradises you had to be at least sixteen years old. I was twelve or thirteen, but even too tall for my age. One July morning I made the experiment. Trembling, fearful, my heart beating violently, I came to a long stone stairway—how broad, how immense, how imposing it seemed! At the top I hesitated for two or three minutes, but finally mustered my courage and entered the application room. I filled out a slip the way I thought it ought to be, and handed it in, with the self-conscious and guilty air of a person who knows he is doing wrong. The clerk—I can see him still, curses on him!—was a little man with a big belly, a pair of squinting watery blue eyes (like the eyes of a dead fish), and deep shrewd wrinkles on either side of his mouth. He looked me over with an air of compassion and, in an irritating drawling voice, inquired:

"Just a moment—how old are you?"

My face flushed with rage rather than with shame, and I answered, adding three extra years to my twelve:

"Fifteen."

"Not old enough. Sorry! Read the rules! Come back in a year."

I went out angry, humiliated, crushed, aflame with a child's hatred of that detestable man who was barring me, a poor boy starving for knowledge, from the use of—a million books, and who, taking cowardly advantage of a mere number printed on a piece of paper, was basely robbing me of a year of light and joy. On entering I had caught a glimpse of a vast hall with lines of venerable, high-backed chairs covered with green cloth, and all around the walls, books, books, books, old books, massive, heavy, bound in leather and parchment, lettered and ironed in gold— a dream! Locked in every one of those books was the thing I wanted, the food for which I was starving: tales of emperors, poems of battles, lives of men who were more like gods, the sacred books of dead peoples, the sciences of all things, the verses of all poets, the systems of all philosophers. The thousand promises contained in those golden letters were for me! At my command those dust-covered volumes waiting there on their shelves behind the closely woven wire of the screening would have come down to me and I could have read them, studied them, devoured them, chapter by chapter, page by page, at my leisure!

I did not wait for another year to pass before trying a second time. Again I failed. Nor was I successful until the next summer. I was then just past thirteen— perhaps thirteen and a half.

With the assistance of an older boy, who for some time had had free access to the library, I was at last able to get in. Fearing that I might attract attention or be taken for a child trying to fritter an idle hour away, I asked for a very serious book—a scientific book—Canestrini on Darwin.

This time another clerk was sitting behind the wood and glass partition—a tall, thin, ungainly fellow, looking more like a plucked chicken than like a man, and so nervous that he could neither stand still nor sit still. Without looking at me he took my slip, marked it with a blue pencil and handed it silently to a fattish sort of boy standing at his side.

I waited for half an hour, holding my breath for fear the book might not be in the library or that they might decide not to bring it to me. When at last it came I clutched it under my arm, and stole bashfully, on tip-toe, into the great reading-room. Never had I been filled with such awe, not even as a child in church. As though appalled at my own daring and frightened at finding myself, after so much plotting, in that im- mense reliquary of the wisdom of the ages, I sat down in the first unoccupied chair I came to. Confusion, pleasure, stupor, the feeling that all of a sudden I was somehow older and more of a man, filled me with such bewilderment that for almost an hour I could not understand a word of the book that lay in front of me.

An atmosphere of majesty and holiness pervaded the great hall—like the sanctuary of a nation it seemed to me. Those chairs, with their dirty, greasy, faded upholstery—the green ending in yellow in some places or disappearing under black spots and stains in others —became in my eyes so many majestic thrones. The silence weighed on my soul more solemnly and impressively than the deep peace of a cathedral.

From then on I went back every day, snatching every hour my tedious school work left free to me. Little by little I became accustomed to that silence, to that great room which soared above my shock of tangled uncombed hair, to that boundless wealth of volumes, old and new, of newspapers, reviews, pamphlets, atlases, manuscripts. Soon I felt quite at home. I came to distinguish between the different employees, to know the meanings of the mysterious numbers on the books and in the catalogues, to recognize the faces of various faithful and devoted bookworms who came there to read, as I did, every day—punctual and impatient as to a rendezvous with a beautiful girl.

I threw myself into all the readings suggested to me whether by my bubbling curiosity or by the titles of books which I found in other books seen in shop windows or on the push-carts of street venders. And so, without experience, without plan, guidance, or direction, but with all the ardor and fury of passion, I began the hard, the glorious life of one who would know everything.

Chapter 4: From Everything to Nothing

WHAT did I want to learn? What did I want to do?
I did not know. I had no programs, no advisers, not
even a definite purpose. What matter whether I
started here or there, turned East or West, went toward
the depths or toward the heights? All I wanted was
to know, know, know—know *everything*. (Everything! the watchword of my perpetual undoing!) Even
at that age, I was one of those men who have no use
for a little or for a half. Everything or nothing! And
I have always wanted everything—an everything which
neglects and excludes nothing. Completeness and
totality, leaving nothing to be desired thereafter!
Finis; in other words, immutability, death!

Eager to know everything and not knowing where
to begin, I flew from subject to subject with the aid
of manuals, text-books, dictionaries, encyclopedias.

The encyclopedia was the height of my ambitions
and dreams; I thought it the greatest of all books; for,
taking appearances and claims at their face value, it
contained—yes, just so!—*everything:* the names of all
men, all cities, all animals, all plants, all rivers, all
mountains, each in its proper place, explained and
illustrated. The encyclopedia answered every question
offhand, without putting you to any trouble of research. My lively imagination pictured all other books

as rivers pouring their contents into that boundless ocean of knowledge; as bunches of grapes destined to fill that great vat of wine with their blood-red juice; as uncountable grains of wheat, which, ground and kneaded, became bread to fill all hungry mouths and satisfy all appetites.

As the mystic loses himself in the thought of the one universal God and seeks to forget all particulars of sense, so I plunged headlong into that sea of knowledge which no sooner flooded my soul than it sent a new desire, a new thirst, upon me.

Through the continued use and handling of encyclopedias I was finally possessed with the idea of compiling one myself. At fifteen, with a mind lusting incontinently for knowledge, the undertaking seemed an easy one. However, my encyclopedia was not to be like others. After a considerable amount of study I came to the conclusion that no complete and perfect encyclopedia was as yet in existence. Some, I found, contained things which others lacked: in spots they said very little, in others much more; and to my eventual astonishment and great chagrin I discovered that in many cases—cases of rare names and information of detail—they were silent, not to say ignorant, entirely.

So I proposed to compile an encyclopedia which would not only contain the materials of all the encyclopedias of all the countries and in all the languages of the world, but go far beyond them all, gathering together in one place information now scattered through many works—not a mere copying and rehashing of old encyclopedias, but a new one based on dictionaries, manuals, and the most up-to-date and specialized treatises on science, literatures, histories.

This decision reached, I did not sit with my hands folded. My life at last had found a purpose. My long hours in the library had now a worthy and a definite objective in view. I set to work with fiery impatience. From that day on—it was July, and my vacation time at school—every word beginning with the letter "a" had for me the fascination of a friendly face. All those solid and compact encyclopedias, lined against the walls, all the big dictionaries, all the much-handled and thumb-worn indices, special lexicons, and thesauri, were taken down from their shelves and brought to my seat in the great hall that I might copy, rewrite, translate, devour them, with an avidity and eagerness even more intense.

Oh, what a nuisance those slimy German rivers beginning with "Aa"—they gave me no end of trouble! What a long list of titles had to be copied before I finished with a family of learned Dutchmen named van der Aa—! How endless and how tedious the enumeration of Latin abbreviations commencing with the letter A! But what a flood of tenderness came over me when I reached the far distant city of Abila that lay by the sea. I met books of law, for the first time, in compiling a self-satisfied treatise on a big word I was delighted to learn: *abigeato*—"cattle stealing." I read the Old Testament in search of Abigail, the pious, and of Abraham, the patriarch; I delved into the com-

mentators of Dante to unearth the life and crimes of
Bocca degli Abati, the incendiary. I became an authority on the history of Abbiategrasso and on the
geography of Abyssinia.

I began by copying confusedly into note-books or on
odd scraps of paper, later rewriting everything neatly
on clean sheets, ruled and margined, which I bound
with string. In the daytime at the library I just scribbled and scribbled—anything would do: my most hasty
and ill-formed letters, with ink spots, abbreviations,
cancelations, scrawls; but in the evening, at home,
under the trembling light of a candle in my bedroom,
my most careful and elegant "English round"—ink red
and black, and a blotter under my left arm! What fun
it was! No game, no ticket to the theater, could have
attracted me away from that dim light where I sat
hunched up over my encyclopedia; it is safe to wager
that even the chance to see some wild animals in their
cages at the fair—an excitement I loved above all
else—would have had no effect on me at such moments.

But this undertaking—which so greatly magnified
me, poor ignorant child that I was, in my own eyes,
and even in the eyes of the library attendants who
looked at me with a certain pity intermingled with
irony and respect—began to lose interest for me, or
rather actually to frighten me, because of the standard
of absolute perfection which I had set myself. I had
been at work at least two months, passing my days
under the sizzling skylights of one library, and my

evenings under the arc-lights of another, or near the candle in my own room; and yet, writing as hard as I could, I had not succeeded in getting beyond the words beginning with "Ad." A long article on the wrathful Achilles bored me; I was skirting the Homeric question—standing on the brink of classical philology: several Greek words (I did not know Greek) baffled and humiliated me.

Reason came to the aid of my fatigue. I was just beginning at that time to dip into philosophy (in who can tell what perfidious books!), beginning after a fashion to think in a more systematic way, thinking much less crudely even than might have been expected of one of my age. Thus I came to realize that true knowledge did not consist, could not consist, in an alphabetical series of facts pillaged here and there and in all directions, nor of a room full of note-books and scraps of paper, mechanically set in order but lacking any breath of life and any thinking soul.

I renounced the idea of the encyclopedia; yet, on the other hand, I determined not to fall into the trap of specialization. My brain, a true Don Juan of learning, refused to concentrate on any one love. Nothing could satisfy me but the limitless, the magnificent, the total of all things, the fullness of the ages, the endless procession of the centuries—and of books.

It occurred to me that history might be just the thing for me.

I thought of history, naturally, on gigantic lines— history of everything, of all human activities (except, perhaps, the sciences, which I could take up later for amusement). I never dreamed, of course, of a short history of any one epoch or any one people; it was to be a world history covering all ages and all races. To be sure, this new decision reduced my original plan by half; but what was left was quite big enough for a writer fifteen or sixteen at the most.

So once again I set out on my way, studying, copying, compiling.

I already knew Cantù's universal history and admired it; for it had come to my aid on many occasions of intellectual embarrassment. But my plan was to write a book that should be more sound, more comprehensive, more accurate. Besides, Cantù was a Catholic and a reactionary. My history would be rationalistic and revolutionary, since at that time I was, like my father, an atheist and a republican.

The idea I had was the antiquated medieval notion of holding up a mirror to all things—but with more understanding and spiritual insight than the historians of old. Facts, facts, facts, all the facts there were, but linked one to another by a growing, an ascending, an evolving life, organized, unified, fixed by human thought, a thought ranging all the way from the blind instinct of self-preservation to the consciousness of the heroic futility of thought for thought's sake!

To begin with I plunged into the morass of Egyptian chronology and came out with an outline of the history of Egypt down to the time of the Alexandrians. I was about to pass on to the Chinese when I suddenly realized that my history was without a beginning! A *com-plete* history of the universe must start with the Crea-tion, not with the first written records merely. My limited knowledge of astronomy and geology had already given me a notion of marvelous antiquities, of perpetual disintegrations and rebirths of worlds. Unlike Cantù, I could not accept, word for word, the Seven Days' Creation of the Hebrews, the "let there be light," and the earthly paradise of "Genesis." The story of the world's inception had to be told, not ac-cording to Moses, but according to S-c-i-e-n-c-e! At that time Camille Flammarion and Charles Darwin represented science to me. The former led me back to Laplace, the latter to Lyell. And so there I was, suddenly turned astronomer, geologist, and anthro-pologist, serving up the world's formation to modern taste. On many a night I strained my poor eyes—already near-sighted—trying to pierce the depths of the sky in search of one of those white nebulæ—vast whirlpools of stars and planets—about which the new cosmologists were spinning such marvelous yarns.

When I had written—with a certain poetic license—the flaming epic of the solar system (and the slower moving history of the cooling of the earth's crust), I suddenly reflected that I still had not done *everything*. I had given an account of the actual facts of the world's creation, but said nothing of what men have dreamed and believed about the beginnings of things—and a history must omit nothing.

So I turned from science to cosmogony; and this

conscientiousness of mine as a fifteen-year-old historian
—not just facts but views and opinions about the facts
—had a great effect on my studies. My curiosity
branched in two directions. On the one hand I came
to comparative literature, on the other to religion. To
religion especially! There was no theogony, no cosmic
myth, that I did not investigate, summarize and copy,
to swell the beginnings of my history.

No religion interested me so much, however, as that
of the ancient Hebrews. We had an old Bible at home
—one of those black covered editions which English
Protestants were offering here in Italy thirty odd years
ago, at half a *lira* (and no takers!); and in it I reread
all of "Genesis." The story did not satisfy me. At
the library I got out the best known critiques on the
Seven Days' Creation, apologies of Catholic "con-
cordists," and heretics on the other side. I made my
way through the long-winded notes and glosses of the
polyglot Bibles. I skimmed, or read, witty and wicked
pamphlets of the eighteenth century and seminary
exegeses sauced in modern style to meet demands of
candidates for the clergy who were not wholly dunces.
I gloated over essays by Frenchmen, as clear and
sparkling as champagne, and over monographs by German philosophers and "higher critics" as solid, as
meaty, and as heavy as loaves of unleavened bread.
And still I was unable to distinguish the truth from
the sophism, the proved fact from the hypothesis. I
also took another peep into the green volumes in the
basket-library; and little by little I forgot the original

object of my research, to lose my way in the labyrinth, the tanglewood, the Slough of Despond, of Biblical interpretation.

I took quite a fancy to the concordistic theory and had the patience to wade through the mountainous volume of a certain Pianciani, and after that the huge *Hexameron* of Stoppani, going on to other biological and scholastic disquisitions by various Jesuits bitten by the Darwinian bug. I remember that one observation occurred to me: all known commentaries on the Bible were made by priests, bishops, theologians, believers, bigots, whether Lutherans, Quakers, Waldensians, or Socinians. Lacking, however—so I believed, that is—was a commentary on the Bible made by a rationalist, by a man capable of viewing facts dispassionately, by a disinterested unbeliever, by a free unbiased spirit, one who would go through the Old and the New Testaments verse by verse and courageously bring to the bald light of day the errors, contradictions, lies, absurdities, proofs of cruelty, deception, rascality, stupidity, with which those pages said to be inspired by God are crammed. Such a commentary would, I thought, do more to undermine faith than all those atheistic philippics, all those dull pedantic controversies which comprise the greater part of modern anti-theology.

"This commentary does not exist," said I. "I will write it!"

By this time gigantic undertakings were failing to give me even a thrill; in comparison with the encyclopedia of encyclopedias this new book was a trifle which I could toss off, so I thought, with the greatest ease— in a couple of years, at the most. I set to work in earnest.

My first step was to get a Hebrew grammar; and in a few days I was writing large distorted letters of the Hebrew alphabet with some speed and copying verses of the Pentateuch from the original. Soon I had what seemed to me a huge pile of notes; and every morning and every afternoon the pile grew higher, till one day I thought I had enough. All this disheveled and unkempt erudition was getting on my nerves. I realized that I must be working it into some sort of shape at once, or I would be dropping it for good and all.

So I wrote out the first verse of "Genesis" in Hebrew and began to set forth my commentary: "On the first day God created the heaven and the earth." But I immediately found myself floundering around in the midst of the biggest difficulties. This single verse contains two words which have always given the commentators much to stew about:—the Christians, in particular, translating them in their own manner to fit the theology laid down in the councils and by the fathers of the church. Does the text say "God" or "the gods," "created" or "formed"?

That is to say, were the first Jews monotheists or polytheists? Did they believe in a creation out of nothing, or did they think of God as a sort of sculptor who merely gave form to an unshapen substance not created by Him and independent of Him? Knotty problems, I need not say, problems involving history, philology, philosophy! But I was not dismayed. I began to write.

I wrote, and wrote, and wrote; but still I could not get free of the mess; arguments pro, arguments con, assertions, denials, affirmations, rebuttals, piled up; quotations in three or four languages followed each other; philosophical and theological parentheses were opened, expanded, but rarely closed! My poor smattering of Hebrew was of little avail in this terrible crisis; I was forced to fall back upon the knowledge of others; and the only dependable authorities, in my judgment, were those who always put the priests in the wrong and gave the verdict to Reason!

I was inclined to believe that the correct translation was "the gods formed"; but how convince others of that—convince them in such a way that they could not answer back? So again I wrote, and wrote, and wrote; but I never could get beyond that infernal verse of "Genesis" which will stick in my memory to my dying day. The more I wrote the more jumbled my ideas became. My brain was a whirl of glosses, etymologies, inductions, reservations, witticisms, which rioted together in a wild dance of hobgoblins to which I could find no rhyme nor reason. At last, at last, I got to the end. I had covered more than two hundred pages in a closely written hand. I was ready for the second verse: "And the earth was without form and void; and darkness was upon the face of the deep.

And the spirit of God moved upon the face of the waters." Here the pitfalls were not so numerous and the theologians fewer, but I still had many difficulties to cope with. I had to explain all that darkness and all that deep and to distinguish between the "spirit of God" and the "idea of God" (the basis of the Alexandrian trinity, this latter). The reference to "waters" brought me to early thinkers of Greece: to Hesiod and his theogony with the world rising out of the ocean; and to Thales, the sage of Miletus, who saw in water the first principle of all things. I was now splashing up to my neck in learning, even venturing a quotation now and then in Greek (what a thrill as I first set my trembling uncertain hand to copying letter by letter words in the divine characters of Plato!). I wandered about in that wilderness of annotations, criticisms, elucidations, dissertations much as Adam must have done in his own private zoo and botanical garden at Eden.

By dint of fast writing I came to the third verse: "And God said: let there be light. And there was light"—words that astounded even Longinus, the rhetorician, pagan that he was, when he came to them. But I was fresh from Bayle, Voltaire, and the author of the *Veglie Filosofiche Semiserie;* I felt no respect for them whatever! Rather it was amusement. What a joke on old Jehovah who was trying to palm His light off on us, forgetting that He hadn't yet made the Sun!

I never got as far as the fourth verse—I was already

tired and bored. If three verses—properly done—took so much explaining, what would I need for the thousands and thousands and thousands of verses in the whole Bible? It was better to go back to the old method of summing up and then attacking. I worked out a plan for a great polemic against faith in general and even went so far as to write several fragments of it out. It was, I remember, in a racy Tuscan style, with a tone of bantering, somewhat in the vein of Guerrazzi's "Ass," which I was reading at that time with inexpressible relish.

My "summa" of rationalism did not, however, get along very fast, because of the competition it suffered from other investigations I had undertaken at the same time, and which derived, like my excursion into higher criticism, from the famous first chapter of my still uncompleted history of the universe. I was so deeply interested in the cosmographies I had found in scriptural writings and in popular myths that I was eager to know more about the poetical forms they had assumed in more civilized ages; so, since I never did anything by halves, I had thrown myself upon the world's literature, hunting down with the aid of histories and dictionaries such poems as dealt with the creation of the world. There were many of them. I read and copied them, as usual, deciding—as usual—to write a book on the subject. One poet after another enthralled me; I would pass on to their other writings, then to their contemporaries, until at last I was as infatuated with Oriental and Occidental literature as I had previously been with the history of the world and with Biblical criticism.

A history of all the world, of all human happenings, is too much, I thought—especially for a novice like me; but I can write a universal history of literature, not, as has been done up to the present time, by nations and century by century, but theme by theme.

I determined on a comparative history of the world's literature that was to be not only bibliographical, but arranged according to substance and subject matter. A vast research, therefore, of indexes, catalogues, titles; countless notes on legends and poetic motives; drawers full of *fiches*. My scope was now somewhat narrowed, but it was still broad enough to satisfy my hankering for the universal. After some months of zealous and disordered exploring I came to realize that again I had undertaken a task too big, too beset with difficulties, to be brought to a happy conclusion. To execute my plan would have required the knowledge of many languages and tens and tens of years of uninterrupted reading. A history such as I dreamed of was not a matter of titles galore; I would have to study the books themselves, read them page by page and several times, to discover sources and establish comparisons.

Another renunciation forced upon me—my fifth or sixth fiasco. So I resolved to confine myself only to the literatures most closely related to my own, the literatures of the Romance languages. Of these I would write a comparative history with an ultimate view to teaching them.

So I blossomed out as a desperate and persistent Romance philologist. I was a great reader of philological reviews, a great decipherer of manuscripts, an assiduous auditor at special lectures, and a demon for handbooks, *Grundrisse,* and bibliographies. I got a fairly systematic view of French and Italian literatures. But I was most attracted by the least known and appreciated of the Romance languages, Spanish. Some time before, through a small grammar for which I had paid three cents, I had learned to read Castilian and had even translated several scenes from "The Marvelous Magician" (*El Magico Prodigioso*) of Calderón. But now I took the books of Amador de los Ríos and of the American, Ticknor, as my guides. I dug up "earliest texts" from the *fuero* of Avila to the latest *romances.* I racked my brain over "The Mystery of the Magian Kings," and was charmed by the *Poema del Cid.* I specialized on Gonzalo de Berceo, the monk, and steeped myself in the savory wit of the Archpriest of Hita. Nor did I stop there: I examined, and read in part, all the volumes of the *Biblioteca* of Rivadeneyra; I unearthed Catalan, Castilian, and Portuguese manuscripts; I almost mastered "old" Spanish; I considered making a number of "critical editions." Books which I was unable to buy, I copied by hand, entire; and at last—the usual ending and one more defeat—I abandoned my idea of a comparative history of Romance literatures in favor of a complete and perfect manual on the history of Spanish letters.

Of this too I wrote the first chapters. I went back

to the Iberians and the Romans. I followed the adventures of the Goths, the invasions of the Arabs, the rise of the vulgar tongue. I actually got down as far as the "earliest documents." I broke off my narrative when my critique of the *Poema del Cid* was in full swing. Other thoughts, other studies—thoughts and studies having little to do with erudition—had come into my head. My history of Spanish literature was my last adventure as a compiler and a scholar—a deplorable adventure, the last phase of a degeneration of the catastrophic rapidity of which I had not been aware.

From the universal to the special, from unlimited knowledge to a universal history, from a universal history to a critique of religion, from higher criticism to a comparative history of universal literature, thence to a comparative history of Romance literatures, and ultimately to a single literature, and to practically one period of that literature. Through partial failures, exclusions, curtailments, restrictions, I, who had set out to know everything, to teach everything, had come to a point where I was proud and satisfied with insignificant quibbles of philology and bibliography, not only in a single furrow, but in a small corner of a single furrow—I, to whom the whole unplowed field had seemed too little for my eager desire to labor!

And all my life, even in later years, has been the same—a perpetual reaching out for the Whole, for the Universe, only to fall back to Nothing—to a humble seat on the grass behind a garden hedge. My life has been a succession of vast ambitions and hasty renunciations. This brief account of my boyish efforts is one among the possible explanations of the secret of my life.

Chapter 5: The Triumphal Arch

I WAS born with the disease of greatness in my brain.
My memory goes back particularly to a time when I
must have been eight or nine years old. I was keeping
very much to myself in those days and spent many an
hour over a stupid school book, full of wretched illustrations and daubs in a violet-colored ink. In it one
day I came across a narrative of Petrarch's coronation
at the Capitol in Rome. I read and reread the story.
"Me too! Me too!" I cried to myself, without even
knowing just why a crown was crammed upon the head
of the fat and stodgy poet. Nevertheless, the round,
ill-drawn face of the lamentful sonneteer seemed to
look up from the dirty page and smile encouragement
at me from beneath its cleric's cowl with the halo of
pointed leaves.

I moved heaven and earth to get my father to take
me to the *Viale dei Colli;* and up there one day I
plucked a couple of branches from an evergreen I
found. I was not quite sure it was the far-famed
laurel—but that detail mattered little. When I reached
home I shut myself up in the little garret at the rear
of the house—the one containing the basket-library. I
wound the branches into a wreath and placed it on my
head; then throwing a large piece of red cloth over my
shoulders, I began circling round and round the room,

keeping close to the walls, chanting a long rigmarole
that I thought sounded tremendously eloquent and
heroic, all the while beating on a wooden box with the
handle of a knife. That was my way of "ascending
the Campidoglio" in pomp and splendor,—the hideous
noise, which I seemed to find indispensable, probably
standing for the applause of an admiring throng. At
any rate, on that gray winter's morning I celebrated
my own mock espousal with immortality.

But the first real promise I made to myself was not
until later, when I was fifteen or sixteen, I believe. It
was about four o'clock on a stifling August afternoon.
Melancholy and alone (as always), I was walking with
lowered head down one of the longest and broadest
streets of my native city. I was tired, bored, discouraged, disgusted with the heat and with mankind.
In my hand I had a newspaper, purchased with considerable embarrassment to my resources.

It was the hour after the *siesta,* when people come
stumbling sleepily out into the open in a foolish hope
of finding a breath of fresh air in the evening cool.
Here were nurses, in white aprons with bows in their
hair, carrying crimson-faced babies that were crying
and squawling in their lace ruffles; here were perspir-
ing husbands with wives clinging to their arms; here
were brothers and sisters swinging along hand in hand;
young men by twos or threes with white cigarettes
hanging from their lips; girls with bright-colored ker-
chiefs on their heads, their flirtatious eyes brimming
with gaiety and mischievous exuberance; old men in

top coats, with blue umbrellas tucked under their arms; and poor soldiers in dark uniforms awkward and self-conscious in the regulation white cotton gloves they were compelled to wear. The crowds grew larger and larger, filling the sidewalks. People began crossing and recrossing the streets, laughing, bowing, calling greetings to one another. Under the rims of great flowered hats the eyes of the women shone like black diamonds. Every now and then small round straw hats were raised above the heads of the multitude in salutation to these beauties.

I was ill at ease in all that animation. I knew nobody and I hated everybody. I was shabbily dressed. I was ugly. My face was pale and stern with discontent. I felt that no one loved me, and that no one could love me. The few who noticed me in passing did not conceal their dislike of me; some, impressed with my truly unusual ugliness, turned for a second look and laughed. I was a special mark for the cruelty of pretty young girls dressed in white and red, with brown skins and pearly white teeth, who were forever raising a laugh behind my back. Perhaps they were not always laughing at me, but at the time I thought they were and suffered accordingly.

All the things that made life beautiful to others seemed to be denied to me. I alone was without love. I alone was without money. If any of these people gave me a thought it was one of scorn. They walked peacefully, indifferently by, caring nothing for the

sufferings of the poor thoughtful youth against whom
they brushed.

Then, all of a sudden, I rebelled. My blood boiled
up within me, my whole being travailed in upheaval.
"No, no, no!" I cried out to myself. "This must not
be! I too am a man! I too must be great and happy.
What do you think you are, you brainless men and
powdered females, who pass me by so contemptuously?
I'll show you what I can do. I shall be more than
you, more than all of you, above every one of you. I
am small, poor, ugly, but I have a soul too, and my
soul will make such a noise that you will be forced to
stop and listen to me. Then I will be somebody and
you will continue to be nobodies. I will create, I will
achieve, I will think, I will be greater than the great—
while you will continue to eat, and sleep, and walk the
sidewalks as you are doing to-day. When I pass, every
one will look at me; beautiful women will have a
glance for me as well; laughing girls will edge close
to me and touch my hand, trembling; and stiff and
dignified celebrities will lift their hats, holding them
high above their heads when I appear; I, in person,
I, the great man, I, the genius, I, the hero."

As these thoughts flashed through my mind I raised
my head; my chest swelled; my eyes, no longer fearful,
looked with pride and hatred into the white and yellow
and brown faces that swept by me. I was a different
person; and I believe that at that moment I was a
handsomer person.

Still under the enchantment of this mood I came into a large open square, where a triumphal arch rose, surmounted by a chariot with galloping horses clean-cut against a flaming sunset sky. I stopped and gazed up at them; and then and there made a vow to myself —a vow that before I died I would achieve FAME!

Chapter 6: Poverty

In those days I was poor, decently but cruelly poor. (I have always hated and I still hate people born with money in their pockets and able to buy what they want when they want it.) Mine was a respectable poverty; I was never cold, never hungry—but I suffered.

It did not matter so much that I wore my father's old clothes—threadbare, shiny, spotted—with invisible patches deftly inserted in the seats and in the knees of my trousers; that my hats had broken rims and crowns; that I wore my shoes until they were too small for me and had been mended and resoled many times. Such pleasures as I had were rare and simple. My childish longings for good things to eat were satisfied with a penny's worth of figs or cherries in summer, and a few roasted chestnuts or a bit of chestnut cake in winter time. Once a year, maybe twice, according as invitations did or did not come, I went to the theater (Punch and Judy) or to a café (ice cream). One Sunday every summer we went picnicking, always in the same place—a string of puddles called a river, dry stones, cane-brakes, sun-scorched meadows, fried fish.

And yet this cheap miserable life of a wretched middle class family gave me no actual suffering except for lack of real money, money of my own, money that

I could spend in my own way for things that I wanted to buy. Those who have fathers in comfortable circumstances and mothers who never say "no"; those who have fat purses in their pockets and penny banks at their bedsides; boys, with appetites bigger than themselves, who have wasted who knows how many lire on whistles, jackknives, marbles, pictures, cakes, bananas, and trash, cannot conceive of my suffering as a child, as a boy, as a youth, up to the time I was almost twenty, for not until then did I have a ten *lire* bill that I could call my own—because I had earned it.

Yet I needed money more than other boys and for quite other things. First of all I needed books—there were so few at home and I had a long time to wait before I was old enough to get into a library; I needed newspapers (from my earliest days those time-killers have lured me); I needed writing paper, pens, ink. Nothing much, to be sure, matters each of a cent or two! But I lacked just that cent or two. My father gave me nothing, and he was right: he had all he could do keeping so many of us fed and clothed. Every now and then he bought a book from some huckster, but never more than two or three in a year. As time went on he gave me an allowance of a *lira* and a half a month (a *soldo*, a cent, a day!)—to indulge my vices—as they say in our Italian families. My "vices" were paper vices—ruled paper and printed paper.

What could I do then? How find the money I

wanted, the money I had to have at all costs to buy the things I needed to keep my soul from starving? I resorted to many devices, first of all to saving. I was given two *soldi*—two cents—a day for lunch at recess. I spent seven *centesimi*. That left me three *centesimi*, which, at the end of a week—there were five days of school—amounted to three *soldi:* the price of one volume of the "People's Library" or three quires of ruled paper. Then there was my mother. She was more merciful than my father—as mothers ought to be. She saw and appreciated my needs. Yet she, poor soul, did not have much more than I—only what my father left her from day to day for household expenses. However, by dint of unheard-of scrimping and saving she found a way to give me two, three, sometimes even four *soldi* a week, four pennies that vanished like magic into illustrated books, ruled paper (ruled up and down as well as from right to left, since then I could get more writing on it), or literary magazines.

I had still a third recourse—stealing; and I am not ashamed to confess it. For many years I cautiously but continuously practised domestic thievery. Under cover of the darkness, in the early morning when my father was still asleep, I would succeed in stealing a few pennies from the pocket of his vest that hung on a hook in the hall. Then again I would keep the change from things I was sent to the store to buy—if my father forgot to ask for it. If he didn't forget, I would tell him I had spent more than I really had or that I had lost the money on the road. I would get scolded on such occasions but I thought it worth the trouble; I got so much pleasure from the few pennies I had safely stowed away.

I even tried to earn money, though without much success. I collected wrapping paper and sold it. I gathered peach stones. I bought and sold canceled stamps. But all this was hard work and the recompense very small.

And yet in spite of my economies, my mother's compassion, my cheating, and my honest business ventures, it often happened that I did not have a penny in my pocket—not even enough to buy a newspaper. These were the days when I would tear the blank pages from my books or leaves from the exercises at school to get paper to write on; the days when I would pour vinegar upon the sediment at the bottom of my inkwell to get something that would wet my pen; the sad days when, longer than was my wont, I would hang around the street corners reading the half columns of the folded newspapers, or slyly peering into the shop windows at the pages of books that chanced to be open.

Oh! the depth of my sufferings during those days— days gray and cold, days of solitude and hopeless misery! How I despaired when the paper I had was spongy and soaked up my pale ink as if with a malevolent intent to confuse words and thoughts; when the point of my pen (the only one in the house) would break and refuse to move across the paper; when I would meet a stubborn bookseller who would not give me a book for a penny or two less when I had just too little money to pay the full price.

In spite of subterfuge, entreaty, deceit, I was always the poor boy, the poor silent boy whom no one likes to have about. In the book stores they paid but little attention to me when I asked the price of a book; for they knew in advance that I had *centesimi*, not *lire*, to spend; the hucksters did not like to have me hanging about looking through their wares and reading furtively as I did so; for most of the time I bought nothing, or at best loose odds and ends that went for little or nothing, or even volumes with pages gone. Newsdealers always scowled at me, because I was always trying to read their papers on the sly without buying one.

I recall with unfailing pride the many humiliations of those years. How many times I passed up and down in front of a show window looking adoringly at some longed-for book, not having the courage to ask the price of it! How many times I felt of the pennies in my pocket, counting them over and over for fear of having fewer than I thought or of having lost them— at last, timidly entering the shop, and standing silently, my face pale, until the proprietor was alone, before I dared to breathe the name of the author, the title, of the book. They all looked down on me in those days, booksellers, their clerks, my schoolmates, my relatives, everybody. I was an ugly, lanky boy, taciturn, ill-clad, with squinting near-sighted eyes, my pockets bursting with papers, my hands dirty with ink, my mouth drawn down on either side with heavy furrows of pain and anger, my forehead already cut with its deep vertical wrinkle.

And yet what did I ask for? Was it to be dressed up like the model boys of the pious illustrations, with neat clothes and starched turn-down collars? Was it to fill my stomach with big meals and sweets between meals to the point of vomiting or bellyache? Did I ask for castles to live in, trips to the resorts, guns, wooden horses, or puppet shows?

I was ugly and repulsive, that I know, as I knew it then—yet underneath that ugliness and that suffering there was a soul that wanted to know, to know the truth, to bask in the sunlight, and steep itself in the sunlight, of beauty; and under that greasy hat and under that uncombed hair there was a mind eager to grasp every idea, every secret, every dream, a mind that already saw what others did not see and found milk and honey where the majority found emptiness and desolation. Why did no one understand and give me something it was my right to have?

However, I do not regret all that misery; nor am I ashamed of my past humiliations. A life of ease might possibly have made me less courageous, less intense, and in the end, far poorer. The unceasing bitterness of one who has nothing, and cannot hope to have anything, held me aloof from others, forced my soul through the mill of pain, polishing it, sharpening it, rendering it a worthier steel.

Chapter 7: My Tuscany

I owe my soul, my spiritual being, to the trees and to the mountains of my native soil no less than to books and to minds of the past. The country has been as much of an education to me as any library. A definite, a particular stretch of country, I mean; all that is poetic, melancholy, gray, solitary in my nature, comes to me from the rural landscape of Tuscany, from the hills and fields that lie about the city of Florence.

Every Sunday, from the time I could walk, my father, a man of few words but of mental attainments far superior to his station in life, took me for a jaunt *fuor di porta,* "beyond the gates," as we say in Florence. We would start off after dinner, alone, never exchanging a word. He knew certain out-of-the-way paths where we could idle along by the hour, rarely meeting a soul. Once in a while a priest, a peasant, or an old woman would come along; but a greeting, a wave of the hand, and we went our ways.

Father was almost always silent and distraught, while I would be turning over one of my precocious fiascos in my mind or ingenuously elaborating some new idea. But I had eyes in my head, and they were open. From over the tops of the walls flanking the road hung tangled branches of gray olive trees; wild roses, dwarfed, neglected, twined their way over the

47

sides, the faded withered blossoms dropping their petals one by one to rot in the ditches below. How many miles I walked along those walls—walls that I can still see before my eyes; low walls that almost invited one to sit down on them; damp walls spotted with lichens and emerald-colored mildew or stained a shining black where the water seeped through cracks; high walls with great black trees, broadening out into heavy foliage at the tops—props, as it were, for some magic hanging garden. Just outside the city the walls were new, freshly stuccoed and ornamented with rustic designs such as common bricklayers might think of. Every now and then we would come to the gate of some villa —gates tightly locked and barred, with watchdogs leaping, barking, at us; open gates with cypress trees like sentinels standing guard on either side and, beyond, paths sloping upward between laurel and myrtle bushes. Here and there the walls came to an end and hedges of tall live-thorn bushes filled the gaps, white with frost and snow in the winter, white with blossoms in the springtime, and in the late summer black with thimble-berries. Still further on, the walls and hedges disappeared and the road, deserted, stony, like the convent roads of mountain regions, wound its way upgrade among cypresses and pines. At last I could look downward, and I would see deep valleys, dewy fields, misty distances, an illusion of the Infinite, in short.

For me it was all like a new birth. Up there, only up there, with the wind in my face, bareheaded, my hat in my hand, with no definite thought in my mind,

I felt that I was living as I should have liked always to live. No sooner did we turn down toward home again than again sadness would settle on my heart, and the deepening twilight, with its far-off, almost inaudible ringing of bells, would intensify my melancholy with waves of pungent anguish. Not to lose the spirit of freedom and freshness of that world entirely, I would always take a piece of it home with me; a wrinkled, shiny black olive found deep down among some leaves; an acorn in its rough cup; a chip of stone, jagged and sharp like some Alpine mountain ridge; a hard green pine cone; a tuft of pine needles; cypress berries; a chestnut; a gallnut. I loved everything that was simple and rugged, things that breathed of solitude and harshness, of a life that was wholesome and in no need of hot-houses or gardeners.

I was not born for the rich and luxuriant countries of the South or of the tropics, for brilliantly colored and highly perfumed flowers, for over-luscious fruits, for sunshine. The country that I love, the country that I *feel*, is my own country, the campagna of Tuscany, where I learned to breathe and to think. A poor, a bare, a gray, a silent country, without adornment, without flamboyant colors, without pagan perfumes and pagan garlands—and yet so intimate, so friendly, so well suited to delicate sensibilities, so congenial to the meditations of lonesome souls! A country monastic, ascetic, Franciscan in its harsh, its black severity, ill concealing its bony skeleton under a robe of green! A country where great, bare brown mountains rise abruptly, almost menacingly, over smiling fruitful valleys—the sweet and sentimental country of my childhood, the solid, stimulating, moral country of my youth! Oh, my Tuscany! In the strong, sturdy, serene baldness of your rocks, with your simple straightforward wild flowers, with your courageous cypresses, your stern oaks, your stinging brambles, how much more beautiful you seemed to me than the far-famed countries of the South, with their palms and their oranges and their figs and their white dust shining under a raging summer sun!

We went out in all seasons; but when my memories are most vivid I see only winter, autumn, and rainy springtimes: biting winds, skies overcast, unbroken, dense and gray; the cold, frowning serenity of an earth that is toiling and brooding in its depths. I never see sunshine; I never feel warmth; occasionally I see a misty, weepy sun peering through a gap in racing clouds to make the dark drear earth darker and drearier than it was before. I see my country as under a cold northern sky, with the grim meditative calmness and solitude of the dying year, when the last forgotten leaf has curled and shriveled on the dried branches of the vines.

I well remember short windy January and February days when we walked away briskly up hard frozen roads that resounded with our footsteps, the walls on either hand sending back the echoes, under a sky flecked with streamers of high white cloud. I would come back home, my feet tingling, my cheeks aflame from the long hard marching, vigorous and vibrant as if I were returning from a victory. But then our dark miserable house, my cold disordered room—a sort of morgue it seemed to be in the dim light of one tiny brass lamp—would plunge me back into a sense of mediocrity, slavery, death. I would pick up a book and begin to read by that faint sepulchral light. Inch by inch my body would grow cold, my feet numb, my gloom more and more despondent, till I would throw myself on my bed to bury in slumber all my unexpressed desires, all my vague yearnings, for a life utterly unlike the life about me—and, for that matter, utterly unlike any other life.

"I left forever the life of the lowlands."
                                    IBSEN.

Chapter 8: I Discover Evil

MY wild and precociously introspective childhood; my
morose and vengeful aloofness from people—born of
my shyness, my "peculiarity," my poverty; the oft-
repeated defeats suffered by an encyclopedic method
conceived on too ambitious scales; my mournful, ele-
giac day-dreaming, indulged, to a vice, on my walks
along gray roads, between blackened walls, beneath
leaden skies; my confused outreachings toward a life
that should be heroic, worthy, full of beauty and poetry
—impulses that were immediately thwarted, stifled by
the hideous, humdrum, every-day reality of a petty,
narrow, cramped, mortifying, provincial existence,—all
developed into a desperate, uncommunicative pessimism, as frowning and self-contained as a fortress without windows. As the boy was becoming the man in
me, my intellect too became of age, demanding an ac-
counting of life—and receiving no answer. Theory
supervened to give form to my melancholy. The sadness—physical, absolute—of those Sunday afternoons
of winter was followed by a searching inquiry into the
evils and the goods of existence. The spirit within me
answered "no" to every promise, "no" to every false
dream, "no" to every specious pleasure, blowing with
a chill breath upon my last lingering illusions as the

55

midnight wind blows on the last flickering flame of an unfilled street lamp.

The languor of long vigils spent in feverish reverie —when people try to pity themselves, quite beyond reason, as they will never pity any other living soul!— prompted a deep searching into the nature of pain and the brevity of our joys, striking a balance between earthly happiness and unhappiness. Tearful sonnets on sunsets and on the sadness of autumn gave way to a firm determination to cry out publicly and rationally against a sheep-like acceptance of life.

At that time the perennial foolish question propounded itself to me in the same terms and in the same way it has recurred in all ages to all souls weary of the world: Is life worth living?

What could I answer? Life promised me little and was giving me nothing. I could not hope for riches nor for success in a profession, since, from the very start, force of circumstances had limited me to a few years of mediocre schooling; I could not hope for the love of women because I was ugly and shy; I could not hope for unlimited learning, for my many thwarted undertakings in that direction pained and dismayed me. Few people paid any attention to me at all, and no one loved me except my father and mother—worlds removed they were from the soul which they had created, a soul that must have seemed a total stranger to them.

Nothing was left to me but thought; I had always liked to generalize, to associate apparently unrelated facts, to divine laws, to pull theories to pieces and put them together again. A short time before, fresh from Vico's "New Science" (which I had imperfectly understood), I had decided to write a philosophy of the history of literature; for I imagined that I had discovered the secret of the ebbs and flows of art, the causes of growths and decays in literature. Even at that early age I was under the spell of Taine, who was opening new vistas to my mind, filling me with envy for the facile art he had of building up clear, orderly, symmetrical systems of ideas with a fact or two thrown in for shading between the lines. Already the demon of theory was lying in wait for the young poet in me, stuffing my mouth with sweeping statements, broad judgments, inferences and inductions faultlessly reasoned with all their corollaries.

So I set my thinking machine to work upon this miserable thing called life—a joyless life that knew no carnivals of happiness, a life as yet uncharted, without beacons, without guide-posts. And it did not take me long to discover its emptiness and its smothered anguish. Was that all there was to it? For every desire a rebuff, for every aspiration a denial, for every effort a slap in the face, for all that craving for happiness which a boy of sixteen or eighteen feels, a promise of —nothing. Nothing! Nothing masked under a hundred disguises! Faith, fame, art, achievement, paradise, victory—so many masks for a reality of despair— eye-holes without eyes, mouth-holes without lips, kisses without requital!

Life to be bearable must be lived intensely. Through it a continuous stream of emotion passes. Though that emotion is ever changing as flowing water changes, it at least bears us along on a current that gives the illusion of continuity and permanence. But analyze life, tear its trappings off, lay it bare with thought, with logic, with philosophy, and its emptiness is revealed as a bottomless pit; its nothingness frankly confesses to nothingness, and Despair comes to perch in the soul as the Angel perched on the sepulcher left empty by the Son of God.

So it happened with me; and with all the ardor of a growing youth I fortified myself in a negation of life. My response—the only one possible at the time—to the wicked injustice of my lot, to the cold and silent hostility of men, was a confirmed belief in the infinite futility of all things, in the congenital rascality, the complete and irremediable unhappiness, of the human race.

My pessimism, though I proclaimed it and believed it to be of a most thoroughgoing kind, was not, how-ever, consistent and did not go as far as it might and should have gone. It was, at first, sentimental, poetic, literary. The inveterate encyclopedist and the bud-ding bard within me divided the task between them. My discovery of life's unhappiness became, in its turn, a pretext for new compilations. As I read I collected the outbursts of poets, the "lines" of dramatists, the epigrams of orators, the admonitions of preachers, the aphorisms of philosophers (and pseudo-philosophers), which, directly or indirectly, explicitly or by implication, revealed or lamented the futility of life, the predominance of evil, the pathos of dreams disappointed, of illusions dispelled, of broodings over a past irretrievably lost; the desperation that bends and breaks the soul when we have looked at life from every angle, only to find it a tiny and barely perceptible island in the infinite whirlpool of Nothingness. I gathered together a formidable thesaurus of gloom articulate, in which sarcasms, witticisms, laments, and mournings of men far separated in space, time, and spirit found themselves huddled together in an agonizing chorus of human discontent.

It was not merely a matter of literary curiosity either; I was sincere. It gave me confidence to find all that distress and all that cursing in others. I no longer felt alone in the world. I had met brothers at last, men born to be comrades with me—the Consoling Dead. After all, I could not be wrong in my negation! My protest was not merely the cowardly whine of a boy wrecked by impotence and disordered dreams.

I not only made anthologies of sayings and quotations, but I also planned to write a book, *the* book, on life—a book which would bring all men to hold themselves and others and Existence as a whole in a much deserved contempt. It was during those days that I came in contact for the first time with a great philosopher; I skimmed, I read, I pondered Schopenhauer, in selections, in fragments, at various intervals, but deeply enough to understand that a facile mastery of textbooks on geology and evolution was not the topmost height to which a searching intelligence might soar. I attempted to outline a history of Pessimism, and so I spent long industrious days in the study of philosophy, where, as was inevitable, I found other ideas, beside these negative and gloomy ones, to attract my attention and rouse my curiosity.

The bookworm in me was no longer working alone; at his side was a theorist waxing older and stronger. The construction of my system of Pessimism (based on the law that the more desirable ends are just the ones that are of necessity unattainable) was attended by intellectual joys hitherto almost unknown to me. I did not forget, of course, to go to extremes and to encompass totality. I did not approve of Schopenhauer's hostility to suicide. On the contrary I planned to end my book with a stoical proposal of universal suicide—and not merely to be smart; I saw no other way out of it. Individual suicide—well, no! That I found ridiculous, futile. Suicide *en masse*, rather; deliberate, well considered, by unanimous consent! Thus the world would be left all to itself to roll its stupid course through the heavens. I thought of founding a society which would grow and expand simultaneously with the sales of my book. When this League of Disconsolates had converted and enrolled all humanity down to the last man, the great day would finally be chosen, and—*finis!* I had even decided on the means —poison seemed to me preferable beyond dispute.

Nonsense, fancies of a child, if you wish! Yet the

fixed idea that I was to be the apostle of this supreme settlement of the problem of life was, for a time, the only excuse I could find for existence. I consented to live only because of the ridiculous hope I had that ultimately I could make all men die with me.

Chapter 9: Others

I was no longer alone. Toward the end of my teens
I emerged from my somber isolation as a child, which
had been the means of saving my soul from the precocious deviltry of most boys of my age. I too had a
heart. I felt that I had something to say, and I wanted
to say it, to talk, to give some vent to my feelings.
Up to that time all the pent-up affection which permeated every fiber of my being I had directed upon
myself. My own experience had engaged my emotions
—self-pity, compassion for my own unfortunate life,
without purpose, without escape. In many pathetic
verses—wretched things written both in Italian and
in French—I had called on death to come to me, and
I had wept over my imminent and pitiable demise. In
the stillness of the night, meditating on the unhappiness of my lot, which closed every door and denied
every joy to me, I shed hot silent tears; and during
the day the clothes I wore—invariably black—and the
expression on my face seemed to be a sort of mourning in advance for my own funeral.

I was in need of affection. I wanted to feel a hand
in my hand, to be listened to and to listen. I wanted
some friend to whom, in secret, in the ease, in the unforgettable relaxation, of friendship, I could confide
those emotions, desires, and thoughts which cannot be

confessed to mothers or to fathers. I wanted some one of my own age to work with; some one older than I to help me, advise me, keep me from mistakes; some one younger than I whom I in turn could help, guide, and counsel.

I scanned faces, I looked into hearts; but most of the time I found only tolerance or disdain, or even worse—that unpleasant and too facile intimacy of ill-mannered youths—the "bad company" of tradition—who slip their arms through yours and talk to you of women and bicycles. My schoolmates were, to speak quite frankly, unendurable to me: self-satisfied, self-pampering philistines in short trousers; pale-faced, round-shouldered "grinds"; loud-mouthed, overbearing bullies,—not to mention that sleek, detestable, self-righteous sham and ninny called "the head of the class." No, that was not what I wanted. I wanted warm hearts and, above all, active, open minds—boys like myself who did not shine so conspicuously in the class room, but who read, thought, and pondered, who asked unusual questions and played with strange and capricious dreams. There was just one such in my school; but he was a teacher, not one of the boys—a teacher by necessity, a poet by nature. Young and of generous impulses himself, he managed to divine in my features and in my words the soul that said nothing to other people. His coming into my life was like the rising of the first star on a lingering afterglow. He encouraged my poetic tendencies. He sympathized with the motives of my groping, vagrant wanderings

in the field of literary research; and though far wiser
and far more learned than I, he treated me as an equal.
He was the first to recognize a man in the stray child
I was.

But cordial though this paternal friendship might be,
it was not enough to satisfy me. I was looking for
young people, boys like myself. I looked so diligently
that in a few years my efforts were rewarded: I became a member of several "groups," or literary coter-
ies, which seemed to me, in the beginning at least, to
be veritable feasts, veritable paradises, of intelligence.

I first threw in my lot with two students, both older
and more advanced in their studies than I (they had
done Latin and even Greek); and together we organized a sort of literary society called "The Trinity."
We drew up a constitution in due form and named the
officers. Each of us had some title or other in the
organization. A by-law required us, each in turn, to
put forward a thesis in the form of a memorial to be
read and discussed by the remaining two. They, of
course, under penalty of disgrace, were bound to take
the opposite view. When my turn came, I filled a
notebook of more than a hundred pages with a captious
and violent criticism of Manzoni's novel, "The Be-
trothed." The book had always been a bore to me,
since the time when I had spent a whole school year
making a logical and grammatical analysis of the quite
commonplace misfortunes of Renzo Tramaglino and
Lucia Mondella.

That insipid, passionless peasant girl; that cowardly

half-witted priest; that friar who always has a sermon
or a benediction under his frock; that Nameless Knight
who tears around making a terrible noise only to collapse at the whimpering of a bigoted female and get
down on his knees before the oratory of a canny saint
—all bored me and angered me. I did not sense the
pure and truly great art that beautifies many pages
of that too famous novel; and, on the other hand, the
atmosphere of Christian forbearance that pervades it,
its servile acquiescence in the whims of a Lord God,
its summary and exemplary punishment of sinners
coupled with a very moderate rewarding of the good
and the unfortunate, roused all the wrath in my Satanic
and Carduccian soul.

Up on one of the hilltops in "my country"—under
another of those February skies, but this time fair and
cloudless—I read my "slam" at Manzoni; and on
those two boys—who later on became very estimable
and esteemed servants of the State—I made a very bad
impression. They were horrified. What? Was the
youngest of the "Trinity" to be allowed to insult, ridicule, belittle, one of the masterpieces of Italian genius?
Audacity, courage, open-mindedness—very well! but
in their proper places and within proper limits! This
was going too far! The discussion that followed was
more acrimonious and heated than usual. After that I
frequently saw my two censors and remained on speaking terms with them; but "The Trinity" was not mentioned again at that time, nor has it been since.

Not long after, fortunately, I met a man—considerably older than I—who was the direct opposite of those first two. He was a poet (he wrote poetry, that is, in both verse and prose); a musician (he played the flute); a hearty, enthusiastic, cordial, impulsive fellow —with all the qualities which I desired and required in a companion. He knew and liked my favorite authors—Poe, Walt Whitman. He was the first to tell me of Baudelaire. He gave me most marvelous new books to read: Flaubert, Dostoievski, Anatole France.

He lived two lives: during the day he was manager or something in a business office; at night and on Sundays he was an ardent, crazy dreamer. He wrote a great deal and had found a way to get several of his things published in the papers. He introduced me to friends of his, artists, or people who wanted to be artists. Among them was a young and delightfully sensitive poet, rich of imagery, with a languor born of all the melancholies, a Heinean and a D'Annunzian in one, a voracious reader of many literatures and, all in all, a writer to the manner born. He was as tall and slender as a lily stem, pale as a mystic novice, chaste and fragile as a girl—not long after that he died of consumption.

With them, too, I met a mysterious funereal painter enamored of Böcklin; a half crazy violinist who improvised (on the piano) wild triumphal marches; a budding composer, on the perpetual lookout for librettos, singing lessons, and other men's wives.

These were not, as I later realized, men from whom

I could expect to gain much, or who would ever rise to great heights of achievement. Yet they gave me, after my freeze-up in books, my first contact with the warm and palpitating world of art. That little make-believe, small-town Bohemia had representatives from every sphere of mental activity. In them I saw men who were doing things, creating, men who would one day attain glory—and not stiff and wan corpses of pompous celebrities who had long since been laid in their tombs. In my eyes those unknown, yearning, zealous youths, intoxicated with their dreams and tormented by their doubts, would be the geniuses of to-morrow, the conquerors of eternity, the joyous creators of new beauties. I wanted to be one of them, to feel myself a brother, a comrade of theirs in this submerged, subterranean pursuit of success and of beauty.

Every Sunday and every holiday we met at the house of the oldest among us; we drank coffee; we smoked cigarettes (my first!); we spoke with unrestrained sincerity of a new book, of a newly discovered author, of an article, of an opera; we argued, we quarreled, we shouted. Or else, amid frequent outbursts of enthusiasm, the poets among us read their poems written during the week; or the man who played the flute would do a pastoral—exquisite in its monotonous tenderness; or a pianist would execute a fugue of Bach or one of his own compositions.

The firm conviction was implanted in every one of us that we were each destined to glory and greatness. We admired each other without envy or rivalry. We courted deception as to our real merits and asked nothing better than to be humored in our dreams. One of the most hackneyed phrases among us was: "A fellow must drink deep of the Chimera's cup!" Just what kind of liquor that famous Chimera brewed I never knew, though we consumed an extraordinary amount of it every Sunday.

In this group of brethren five I had my small place too: I was critic, scholar, philosopher. They turned to me when they wanted some historical fact, the title of a book, information on some fashionable scientific theory of the day.

They considered my knowledge unlimited, though its only legitimate claim to such distinction lay in its contrast to their ignorance. The name I thus acquired, and my as yet not wholly conquered taciturnity, inspired a greater fear and respect for my authority than safety required, while I in turn was so overwhelmed by their esteem for me that I never ventured to read them any of the things that I was continuously writing on the intricate problems of life and death.

Although I felt at my ease in these periodic hurly-burlies of intellect and poetry, I still sensed that these new friends did not wholly satisfy me, and that my spirit, my mind, already accustomed to abstractions and inclined to systematic thinking, really wanted something else and something more. True, I found pleasure in the warmth of that light and somewhat vulgar enthusiasm. Under the influence of all that poetry my sensibilities had gained in breadth and fineness. Music,

which I had there been enabled to enjoy for the first
time in my life, furnished a more stately rhythm for
my visionary gallopings.

But I could not find in any of my new friends a
love for naked thought, the habit of reasoning, nor any
taste or aptitude for logical fencing. After two years
I betrayed them, little by little, for new companions,
for new cerebral orgies.

They were three, these new ones: a student of medicine (blond and handsome), who preferred Shelley
and Musset to textbooks on psychiatry, and the Uffizi
Gallery to the dissecting room; a quasi-doctor of letters,
a dwarf and a great talker, an indefatigable noser about
bookshops, a poet incognito, at times a braggart and
bluff, but, at bottom, a good fellow; and a "rough-
neck," younger than the rest of us, lacking system in
everything, schooled in no school, a student of no subject, a sworn enemy of all discipline, deficient in self-
confidence (but very proud), a cynic and a pessimist.
I felt at once that this latter youngster had more stuff
in him, more real substance, than either of the other
two, and I attached myself more particularly to him
from the very first. The first day we met I picked an
argument with him, but thereafter we joined forces
against the others. In our daily meetings they stood
for poetry, literature, elegance, *snobisme,* in a word,
for that D'Annunzian spirit which was beginning about
that time to swell the heads and rot the brains of the
prematurely senile youth of Italy. We two, on the
contrary, stood for facts, for definite documented

knowledge, for ideas, for simple and symmetrical theory, for hard and rigid philosophy. For many months the four of us were able to hold together and argue without too much bitterness. Our common sympathies and, above all, the hatreds which we shared, constituted a close bond between us. But soon the pricks and the blows began to hurt: irony quickly changed into sarcasm, innuendo to insult. The ties that bound us were mysteriously weakened; we met a few times in an atmosphere of tragic suspicion. Finally we all agreed to a complete and everlasting separation—two in this direction, two in that. I can still see the street-corner (I even remember the hour of the day) where the irrevocable divorce was consummated. We parted without so much as a hand clasp or a good-by; and when night fell, I found myself with a single friend, my only life-long friend, a friend whom I shared with none.

Chapter 10: He![1]

DEAR Giuliano! More than twelve years have passed since that muggy rainy autumn in which our lost souls met and found each other. Now we can speak of those days calmly, serenely, as if they were lived by two entirely different people—though we still bear the names they bore and have so many memories in common with them.

We are not, in fact, the same people. I am not I. You are not you. A time came when we each went our ways. You are now a grown man, sane, solid, industrious, esteemed; you have admirers, followers, perhaps even disciples. You have fought your battles and you can show your scars; you have created something out of nothing; something that stands up, that passes, that even pays. Under the overalls of a laborer, behind the spectacles of an accountant, you have tried to conceal the pain and torment of your deep, rich, complex soul.

I am still the star-gazing wanderer I was in those days, roaming the universe, rudderless, and without a course. I have, as we Italians say, "neither art nor part"—I belong neither here nor there. Not a stone have I whereon to lay my head—the stone of one definite, reliable resource, I mean. There is no corner

---

[1] Giuseppe Prezzolini.—Translator's note

71

of the earth I can put a fence around and say: "This is mine!" However, I too have changed—and how greatly, how greatly changed!

So we can talk of those years with apparent calm at least, as though it were a matter of history—history of other people. Talk of it, nevertheless, I must; for our friendship was not like other friendships,—frivolous, sentimental, a passing acquaintance. You must agree with me, Giuliano; our friendship was not like other friendships.

I wonder whether you ever realized—realized deeply, in its true significance—what an impressive, what a beautiful thing our long comradeship was? For my part I cannot think of those years of my life without seeing your image rise before me—you, a studious and excitable Jacobin! And I see myself too, and always at your side; now battling, with lowered head, against the sleet storms of winter or against the dust storms of summer; now leaning on the parapets along the Arno watching the fishermen so industriously wasting their time; now lying on my back on the grassy summit of the Mugello; now bending over the pushcart of a bookseller in search of some treasure second-hand; now seated in silence at a bare table in some country tavern. No matter how hard I try, Giuliano, I can never see myself alone. I can remember our long comradeship, day by day, hour by hour; but apart from it, nothing!

Do you remember? Do you remember where you first lived—the house in that spotless, deserted street, tucked away between great residences and gardens so forbiddingly closed, a street where no one ever passed, after dark, except lovers and janitors? (A large house with a yellowish tinge not more than fifty years old at the most, but already with a mellow air of age and sadness!) Do you remember the big dark room you had—filled with books, the treasure trove of countless gems of French and Italian literature, the promised land of my ignorant but insatiable curiosity? Do you remember our long chats in that room while the dry logs in the fireplace crackled cosily—evening falling rapidly outside, and church bells madly tolling *anime* —souls of long forgotten Dead? Do you remember? Do you remember the arid little garden that lay buried between damp walls and closed windows, where for the first time we talked of Stirner and the divine freedom of the Ego? Or do you remember, rather, our climbs up the hills to see the sunsets, looking down on the city squatted in its sodden cowardliness on the banks of the lazy stream, and saying to ourselves: "That place will be ours some day!"?

At times we went further on, up into the mountains, in quest of solitude, of sharp air, of a sterner Nature. The roads never seemed long. We walked on and on with light impatient strides, brightening the journey not with song, but with arguments, thoughts, witticisms. A long hill to climb roused us like a battle to be won; while the down grades brought us silence and humiliation. Soon the city walls were far behind us; soon also the barbed wire fences and the fields—

ruled with straight furrows like the pages of a copy book at school. We wanted highlands, we did! We wanted altitude! Altitude and freedom! Not roads lined with their everlasting hedges, but foot-paths, mule-paths, trails that clipped the curves in the climbing highways. We followed the clearings of the wood lots. We took to the stony slides that led straight up to abandoned cabins! And up at the summit there we halted—under the walls, perhaps, of some wretched convent (all its doors and windows closed) or near piles of stones that once had been a castle; and we sang the "Marseillaise" in the crisp February air, our only audience the empty, disconsolate valleys, the faraway mountains, their slopes black as poverty, their peaks radiant with snow and sunlight under a sky roughened with cloud; and our chests expanded with each panting breath and the violent beating of our hearts. How far away we were from all the noise and stuffiness of the city, from all its holy laws of daily humiliation! We felt that we were alone in the world, masters of all about us, the only worthy and noble men alive! The wind blew, splashing into our faces the few drops of water still clinging to the shriveled oak leaves. Stiff white clouds journeyed past us across the vast colorless sky. Trees groaned, protested, as the ruthless norther beat against them; under our feet the brown frost-bitten grass lay patiently waiting for springtime and the fragrant secret of the first violets!

Dear Giuliano; to-day we are two men, and not two

boys. We have wives and children—responsibilities not a few. We, in a certain sense, have souls in our keeping. And yet, I do believe, if anything not wholly insincere ever came from our hearts, if, after death, something of us is to endure in the lives of others, we shall owe it—as we owed it then—to those chill winter Sundays, to those flights we used to take out toward the naked earth, up toward the pure heights!

Do you remember the evenings when I used to come to your house—your other house—where you would be writing all by yourself, waiting for me? Directly in front of your windows stood a cypress tree, and beyond the cypress a path leading up a hillside. We loved that cypress—a tousled, unkempt tree, dusty with the dust of the city, but black and solitary on that ancient garden mound. And we often looked at the path that went upward beyond it! Our lives were paths that went upward, too—resolved ever to go upward! All our dreams we dreamed in high places—our feet in the moist grass, and the fragrance of bloom in the air! All our plans for books, all our literary manifestoes, all our "programs of action," we first thought of and evolved up there, a thousand feet or more above the level of the sea—and farther still above the level of mankind! And in every one of my plans you had your share, as I had mine in everything of yours. We divided the universe sharply into two parts: you and I on the one side, and all the rest on the other.

Up there, toward the end of Via Leonardo, there were two thick and majestic cypresses of almost equal height. They stood side by side, and alone, apart from all other trees. We said, on one occasion—do you remember?—that those two trees were we two; and that just as their roots twined and intertwined beneath the earth and their branches twined and intertwined above the earth, so we should be united in life and in immortality. We even said that their fate would be our fate: that if one of them were cut down or struck by lightning, so one of us would come to an end. But the two cypress trees are still standing there; no storm has wrecked them; no ax has been put to their roots; the sparrows still sit in the branches at nightfall, twittering their loves. And we two are still alive and still near each other—but mad conceits are no longer buzzing in our brains; and whenever I chance to pass those two black brothers, I lower my head and—I don't know why—I feel a clutch of anguish at my heart!

Don't you realize what a tremendous thing, what a beautiful thing, our friendship of those days was? I don't know whether I still live in your memory as you live in mine; I don't know how far you are conscious that all that was best in us began in those days —and not before; that it was during those very years that our souls, our characters, our personalities, took on their permanent outlines and measured the full stretch of their wings.

We are near each other still; and yet so far, far apart! I know nothing of you and you know nothing of me. But as I picture you seated at the big scrawled and spotted tables of the library—afternoons, during the days of our passionate research—bending over open books, over the paper unfolded in front of you—or hear your voice asking or answering a question (both of us looking around out of the corners of our eyes to be sure the gruff and relentless beadle would not catch us whispering!)—I understand everything: you become mine again, all mine again, even as you were in those far-off days of our impatient toiling.

Then there were the nights—late—when we went to the café, to a table hidden away in the farthest corner under the great iron and glass canopy of the drinking-room. Do you remember how silently and disdainfully we worked our way—our black coats drawn tight about us—through the tables, where families of "fat bourgeois" were seated, or solitary well-fed philistines dying of boredom, hypnotized by the empty glasses in front of them and the chatter of fashionable boys of the town, rich, but so "common"? What a delight for us to steal into our corner away off there, to sip our hot—and wretched—coffee, reviewing the day's acquisitions, discussing the present and the future, making remarks about the half-witted stare of the man at the next table, cataloguing the fortunes of the world, the plagues of the earth, and the hopes of Heaven! How many books we tore to pieces there; how many truths we discovered (rediscovered); how many reputations we ground to powder; how many systems we sent to the junk yard; how many prefaces and indices we wrote; how many smart phrases we aired; how many shafts of wit we barbed! Absinthe, champagne—for us? Ours was the intoxication of divine youth, a drunkenness without wine, an orgy without women, a carnival without music and dancing! Ours was the daily exultant uncovering of our Selves, of our real and innermost Selves: the discovery and continuous remodeling of our minds—minds of poetthinkers, sounding the depths of the universe!

We discovered our Selves; and we discovered Thought, at the same time and together. I revealed your soul to you, and you revealed my soul to me. We believed everything, we denied everything, together. Together we built up. Together we tore down. Side by side, with hands clasped, we sought Truth, devoured books, searched, questioned, throwing the best established, the most undisputed, glories into the crucible of criticism! At the self-same instant we deserted the faith of our fathers, the idols of our tribe, tearing off the muzzles of the timorous. We slept in the same bed. We ate at the same table. We marked the same passages in the same books. And yet, there was nothing soft or effeminate about our friendship, nothing familiar, nothing sentimental, nothing—yes, even this I will say—nothing from the heart. It was the friendship of two tormented brains, not the affectionate communion of two confiding souls. We never wept together—not even once. We never betrayed the intimate secrets of our love affairs. When you became engaged I heard of it from other people; and I got my first announcement of your marriage from the *Corriere della Sera*. Ah, to good purpose, in those days, we were reading *Le Rouge et le Noir* and *La Mort du Loup!*

Yes, you must agree, Giuliano, our friendship was not like other friendships. It was altogether mental, philosophical, intellectual—from the brain—though it had all the warmth and all the trials of true affections of the heart. Indeed I am not quite sure that the heart did not enter into it to some extent. I am not wholly brain. Don't you too feel a certain homesickness in these recollections, a melancholy yearning for a happiness gone forever? Why do these memories of mere walks and mere talks and mere readings—memories of a simple uneventful past of labor and of silence —move me more than the memories of my lost loves? Why do I still feel for you a tenderness which I never voiced and never hinted, which I never showed in my actions nor expressed in my letters? No, I am not at all sure that our hearts did not have their share in our friendship.

You alone could perhaps tell me—but I will not ask you to. I must not let you tell me. That must remain another of those secrets, the last indeed of the secrets, that made our manly comradeship so pure and so wholesome!

Chapter 11: I Discover Unity

Up to that time thinking had served me as a witness and a corroborator of my ill-being, my sadness, my naïve disgust with life, as a crutch, as a buttress, as shoring—nothing more! In a loud voice I called upon philosophy to explain and justify a judgment preconceived; and I praised this my servant, friend, and abetter so long as it proved me right, so long as it lent me authority (at the time I thought it a venerable authority) to clothe, in the face of my antagonists, the poetic nudity of my childish and imaginary woes. My choice of the plain and somber cloak of philosophy rather than—like another Shakespeare—the frilled and flourished mantle of poetry proves, I believe, that I had an instinctive leaning toward abstract thought, and an intuitive recognition that that particular cloak had an intrinsic value, a value superior to that of other cloaks, and that I was already on the way to discovering that under the make-up a living substantial body might eventually be found.

In fact it was through thinking that I escaped from my despondency. Method made me lose sight of results. Means came to obliterate ends. As I have already stated, I was determined irrefutably to prove the essential evil of life—in such a way that it could be denied by no one, that everybody would have to admit: "Yes, that is so! It cannot be otherwise!"

It seemed to me that only science could offer certainty; and so, since it was philosophy I wanted, it had to be a philosophy deeply grounded on the sciences and born of them. Such a philosophy I found—a philosophy that everybody knows. In our day, in Italy, it goes under the name of Positivism.

I set out, accordingly, to make a "positivistic" demonstration of Pessimism. With all the hunger of my eighteen years, I threw myself upon anthropologies, psychologies, biologies, and sociologies— sciences which in those times had reached the untenable meridian altitude which already presages decline. I accumulated facts. I copied statistics. I applied theories. I attempted generalizations; and—apelike—I improvised hypotheses and systems of my own. Bit by bit I began to enjoy the game; I forgot the tragedy of the world, Leopardi's "vanity," Schopenhauer's "renunciation," and my own boundless discontent. I loved research for its own sake. I loved the idea that generates a greater idea—the marvelously widening comprehensiveness of the abstraction. Method and generalization came to possess me; I no longer saw my unhappiness reflected in the world, but began to feel the world thinking in me. From that time on my life was thought and thought only. Ideas—"the idea"— seemed to me the only reality, and philosophy the only perfect expression.

I was smothered in facts, but facts were not enough

for me. No matter how deeply I fathomed them, no matter how many of them I got together, I could never exhaust the Infinite. That wealth of the particular which had been my sole wealth during the days of my disordered erudition seemed woefully meager to me now. My mind eager for vastness and completeness now hungered for universal concepts as the only food able to appease its appetites. Theories excited me more than proofs, ideas more than experiments, and two puny facts seemed to me more than enough to base a system on. Forging ahead in the effort to crowd more and more reality into fewer and fewer principles, I brought up, as was natural and necessary, in Monism—not, of course, the idealistic Monism which I later came to know, but a Monism such as the great mechanists I was then hobnobbing with were likely to inspire. I believed—*believed*, notice—that all the entities of the universe were reducible to a single substance, which, though unlimited, more closely resembled old-fashioned "matter" than anything else.

To me this Monism, this faith in the profound and substantial unity of all things, was not a mere word, a mere phrase, a mere formula. I felt it and I lived it within myself in every moment of my life, the way one lives a great passion or a great love. All things, no matter how diversified, became in reality one thing to me; and this ultimate substance, the substratum of the changing whole, was not an intellectual concept, but reality itself. I got no end of ecstasy from the conviction that I knew, *knew,* that all the objects about me, objects so vastly differentiated and unrelated in the judgment of the ordinary fools I met every day, were to me, on the contrary, one and the same object, referable to one and the same principle, made of one and the same stuff, shaped and colored in a thousand ways for the convenience of our senses.

My faith was so great that I turned apostle. I was beginning at that time to overstep the circles of my schoolmates, frequent the society of older intellects (which were, or seemed to be, superior to mine), or of people not so well read as I, but interested in new ideas, and on whom I could venture my first experiments as a missionary. I shall never forget a certain day (what music! what sunshine!) in the month of June. I was calling on a young novelist (still unpublished) whom I was trying to convert to my belief. All of a sudden the bells began to ring for noon-time, and for a moment the air, already filled with sunshine, seemed to overflow with warmth and sound.

"Just think!" I said to my friend, pointing to a pen. "Just think! This pen here, and the sound from those bells, are one and the same thing. Here you have an energy that is shut up, imprisoned, for the time being, in wood and steel. There you have the same energy running free, expanding in ever-widening circles across the blue sky. Where can you find me a more magnificent and profound truth than that?"

At the moment my whole soul with its five senses was

conscious of that divine Unity. I was acutely, vividly, physically aware of a great whirling of inimical diversities roaring back toward the single fountain head from which they came, and where eventually they would reunite in the unity of a pantheistic Nirvana.

Chapter 12: I Am the World

BUT I did not stop even at Monism. My mind was, as it still is, a vagabond easily distracted from one thing to another. And then thought never stops either. The end of the last page is only the beginning of another chapter, and every peak attained is but the spring-board for a new leap.

No sooner had I made the principle of Unity mine than I was confronted with the question that eternally recurs in human thought: Of what does this Unity consist? Matter? Ether? Energy? Spirit?

I relived, within myself and along its broad lines, of course, the whole drama of philosophy. The affirmations of the early naturalists were met by the obvious rationalistic objections. The universe of water or fire, of corpuscles or vortices, gradually became the world of reason, the multiple incarnation of ideas, the crystallization of the Divine Logos, the changing stream of images, the kingdom of the Spirit Manifest. The idealistic solution won me over. *Esse est percipi!* Immediate reality is sensation. Sensation is an affair of ours, of the human mind. Beyond sensation we know nothing. Sole witness, sole detector, of reality is the fact of continual occurrence and recurrence of *states of mind*, of happenings in consciousness. The world is a creation of our own minds, our own "representation."

My philosopher was no longer Schopenhauer, but Berkeley.

Is there something beyond this representation? Is knowledge a trustworthy window opening on the Real, or is it merely a fabric of ground or painted glass—a translucent crystal affording only false and uncertain shadows of the truth? Is there really something behind knowledge, or is there nothing (as there is nothing behind life)? Is knowledge, perchance, merely the mirror of itself—bark without tree trunk, drapery drawn across a void?

These questions, which a sane man does not ask himself, which the professional philosopher smothers by burying them in long words, troubled me to the depths of my being, forcing my brain to ceaseless antics in a mad hunt for arguments, sophisms, subterfuges, keeping me in a state of feverish anxiety and strain as though my very life depended on my finding answers to them. Now, with the passing of the years, I can see how ingenuous my method of stating the problems was and how crude my solutions of them; but in those days they were matters of grave concern, inner experiences far more important than a first love or an unexpected windfall of money. Thinking was my whole life and the selection of a theory determined the character and outlook of my whole existence.

Every evening, from four to seven and from eight to twelve, there were discussions—discussions with friends, discussions with enemies, discussions in loud voices in utter earnestness and fury. There we were—

walking down along the banks of the yellow river or up along the higher boulevards, jostling our way through crowds of people in town or loitering in and out among the trees in the country; on slippery paving stones of the city, on the white macadam of country roads; under soft hazy skies of early evening; under skies of night dripping with rain, or shivering with sparkling stars; groping along through foggy streets, avoiding the traffic; seeing nothing, hearing nothing, unconscious of the outside world whose existence we denied or affirmed at least once every half hour. Theory of knowledge; perception and representation; objectivity and subjectivity; idealism and realism; Kant and John Stuart Mill; sense and reason; Plato and Locke—the whole arsenal of epistemology was wielded in the fray! We would return home hoarse in our throats, deaf in our ears, our heads muddled, bewildered, dazed, wondering all the time whether this confusion of definitions, arguments, inductions, might not be, after all, the product of a stupid misunderstanding, a simple, ordinary matter of words.

But my idealism held its ground. It seemed to me the only logical premise—and, being logical, it did not stop, in my case, with the usual identification of the external and the internal. The world is representation—granted! But I know nothing of any representations outside my own. The representations of others are as unknown to me as the essences of inanimate things. The minds of other people exist only as hypotheses of my mind. The world is therefore a creation of mine—the world is my soul—the world is—ME.

What a marvelous discovery! What a sudden and unexpected burst of light! No idea ever stirred me and transformed me as this one did. I paid no attention to its wild conflict with common sense; I did not realize that it might be a dialectic equivocation, a juggling of words, and nothing more. The very absurdity of it enkindled the ardor of my faith. No one believes it? No one can believe it? So much the better! *I* believe it. The profoundest truth is always the last to be discovered!

And I believed it with all my brain; I took it seriously, literally, elbowing its remotest and most obscure consequences aside. My life became something fantastic, something divine, though nothing in the world about me had changed at all.

The whole universe was only a part of my Self; its very being depended on me, on my senses, on my mind. Things appeared and disappeared according to my movements to and fro. If I came back, they reappeared; if I left them again, again they vanished. If I closed my eyes all colors died; if I stopped my ears, no sound, no discord, no harmony broke the silence of space. And the ultimate corollary: When I die, the world dies with me! But a last doubt was left: Shall I die as others die? Is it possible that my mind will ever cease to think?

And men! Passing shadows that move across the curtain of my senses, phantoms evoked by my will, pretentious puppets dancing on the stage of my mind's theater! What a joke on them! How much more insignificant and ridiculous they now seemed to me, with all their contortions, than they had ever seemed before! As I passed through a crowd of people I would think: "See these idiots here! They fancy they are living beings, living on their own account and, perhaps even—credulous fools!—immortal! They don't in the least suspect that they are just pictures hastily flitting across the retina of my eye; just memories or expectations of my mind; insubstantial drops in a river of images which rises and empties wholly within my spirit. Not only this: here they are buried in Non-Being up to their necks! Yet just see them strutting around as though a full life awaited them, a life without end!"

And looking at them thus, I smiled and hated them no longer. All the bitterness their former unjust contempt had caused me now vanished from my heart. I was no longer a victim; I had become master and despot. I was the only living soul in a concourse of shadows.

In those days I must have felt somewhat as God would feel if He really existed. I was a tireless Creator and Annihilator. The world lay at my feet; I had only to lift my hand completely to remodel or, more exactly, to reabsorb it. There were moments when this thought filled me with such transcending exaltation that I forgot I was the little Self I had known and endured so long. Of a sudden I had been transfigured, gigantified, like an imperious god, stepping forth triumphant from the husk of a paltry man.

Chapter 13: Nothing Is True—*Tout Est Permis*

THE perfect and logically unassailable absurdity was the maddest form of inebriacy I practised in my early youth, though it had no hang-over to speak of, as is the case with all honest inebriacy.

However, the morning after was, for me, a sad one. Accustomed, finally, to thinking of myself as the axis of the universe, as the only unity capable of giving shape and stability to Non-Being aspiring to Being, I suddenly awoke to the fact that I had been, all along, the dupe of a play on words, the victim caught in a trap of logic, the nut in a metaphysical nut-cracker. All those thrills, all that excitement, all that wonder, over a false deduction in a vicious circle! To say that the world is representation is to say, simply, that representations make up the world—that the world exists. To believe in the existence of other people means nothing more than that certain complexes of sensation—governed by wills similar to ours—exist and are called men. We have simply formulated a few definitions that make no difference to anybody anyhow. We can go on using the same vocabulary as before. We must go on acting as we acted before. My will is still obstructed by physical bodies. Not only that: my will is still obstructed by other wills! Which proves that instead of being a god, I am simply a fool.

Later on this conviction prompted me to seek another road to divinity—by lengthening and broadening the reach of *my* will. Then, however, the disappointment and humiliation of my awakening was so great that I threw myself over to the opposite extreme. I lost all faith in thought, in reason, in philosophy. Thought became paradox in the service of poetry; reason a geometrical symmetrical design of pure line without dimension; philosophy a dialectic expression of the likes and dislikes, of the mental and moral needs, of this and that individual man—not of the universal Spirit Incarnate. Logic, which, with its free autonomous severity, its unswerving restless pace, had been my guide hitherto, now turned into a weapon of subtle, captious, disintegrating sophistry, which I applied with spiteful zest to all possible thoughts wherever the opportunity presented itself. I became a sort of Gorgias of the Florentine cafés—Gorgias, who, to solace himself for his own loss of nerve, for his own broken pride, amused himself by blasting, withering, the self-assurance of other people, demolishing the theories and systems they set up, refuting every positive statement they made, taking advantage, in so doing, not only of their weaknesses or their ignorance, but also of his own bad faith, unfairness and obstinacy. I delighted now in filling the heads of dogmatists with doubts, in silencing enthusiasts, in ridiculing fanatics, in humiliating glib talkers. It was a bitter, malicious, futile form of amusement, but it gave me pleasure. It was the only vengeance within my reach. Deliberately now I sought out people, not to convince them, as I had formerly done, but to unsettle them, bewilder them, make them again like myself.

Very few could hold their ground. A vigorous manner of talking, a gift for speaking offhand, my practice in argument and debate, my ready wit, my knowledge of various philosophies, and a brazen fondness for showing my erudition quickly gave me as a rule the windward position. I had mastered method: I had every manœuver, every trap, every thrust, at my instant disposal.

Everything is relative. Error here is truth there. Truth here is error there. Every principle contradicts itself. All systems of metaphysics are but restatements in different language of two or three general formulas inevitably reducible to some mystic Unity—a unit which cannot be comprehended, which is nothing, and means nothing. Philosophies are made to justify our prejudices, to humor our sentiments, to serve the requirements (even the base requirements) of our practical lives. Translate philosophy into terms of life, and we get something closely resembling Carlyle's outline of the metaphysics hogs would have if they took up philosophy. The only reality is the Now—sensation: let every one live in his own Now, and let formulas and faiths go hang. People should shed the scabs of their old diseases, set themselves free, believe in themselves and in the passing moment, which is a beautiful moment precisely because it is a passing one.

And as I have never stopped halfway in any of my adventures, it did not take me long to deduce the ultimate consequences of this negation of every principle and every rule. I came across Max Stirner at that time and it seemed to me that I had at last found the only master I could not do without. From the intellectual absurdity I passed on to the moral absurdity. There was no other god before me, no other god outside of me. I worked up a sort of Egology—purging my soul of family affection, wrenching loose from all ties that bound me to country, from all restraints of respectability and good manners. I was an anarchist. I proclaimed myself an anarchist. I saw no other purpose worthy of attainment than a complete emancipation of myself—and of others. (For, of course, to demand freedom myself I had to concede it to others.)

With three friends of mine I founded a society of individualists; I wrote a "Manifesto of Free Spirits"—and we were off on a roaring tear—wine, hashish, and ferocious nonsense.

Nothing was sacred in my eyes any longer: even revolutionary agitation and humanitarian reform which at first had seemed to me such grand things now suddenly appeared as childish dreams of ignorant and inexperienced fanatics. It took more than that to satisfy me! I demanded an *inner* ideal, a radical liberation of all men, and of their souls as well as of their bodies—and possibly a stick of dynamite here and there to help hurry things along. With the few kindred spirits to whom I had broached the matter, I considered seizing the city by a surprise attack some night. I began preparing myself for a world revolution. I wanted to get away somewhere, travel in all the countries of the earth, rub elbows with people of all kinds and climes, to have my fill of fragrance in the Orient, lose myself for once in the fogs of the North.

Meanwhile, unable to do one blessed thing, discontented, overwrought, hungry, yet blasé to everything, I vented my rage in irritating epigrams, in mordant cynical explosions in Nietzschean style. In utter contempt of Madame Philosophy and of Kant, her egregious Alfonso, I planned a "Critique of All Reasons"—and a "Twilight of the Philosophers." I felt a missionary's call to free others as—I believed—I had freed myself: with naked and fearless theory!

How was I to do this? Through a periodical, of course!—a publication combining enough science to clear the ground of rubbish, with more than enough of the freakish, the crude, the anti-idealistic, the exotic, that would be furnished by myself and my closer associates.

Chapter 14: Fever Heat

EVERY time a new generation makes its appearance on the stage of life, the world's symphony strikes a new tempo. Dreams, aspirations, hopes, joys of discovery, plans of attack, drum-beats to battle, challenges, impudences—and a magazine!

Every article has the tone and the ring of a proclamation; every controversial shaft, launched or received, reads like the bulletins of a victorious general; every headline is a manifesto; every book-review a storming of the Bastille; every new volume a gospel; every conversation a conspiracy of Catalines or a council of *sans-culottes*. Even private letters have the galloping rhythm of apostolic exhortations.

The man of twenty looks upon the veteran as his enemy; every established idea is suspect; every great man is brought to trial again. History begins to look like an interminable night broken by flashes of lightning, a period of hushed, impatient expectancy, an eternal twilight of dawn, waiting for OUR coming to bring the sun. To the man of twenty even sunsets seem to show the delicate white spangles of lingering sunrises; funeral torches are joyous beacons promising new festiveness; plaints of the tolling church bells are peals of joy announcing new births and summoning to new baptisms. A man's twenties are the one period in his

95

life when he can really swagger, when he has the manly
foolhardiness to take every bull by the horns, when
he can walk with the light and firm step of a conqueror, his hat over one ear, and a walnut cane in his
nervous hand!

To us of the new generation every colored rag is a
battle standard; every squeak or grumble a mighty
convulsion of revolt; every exploding fire-cracker the
first shot of an Armageddon; every sprinkle of rain the
beginning of a second Deluge. With distended ears we
listen to the murmuring of the wind and believe it the
end of the world; the beating of the hoofs of a draught
horse on the pavement makes us run to the window
as though it were the black Bucephalus of the Anti-
christ; and the rays of the setting sun make us almost
see a hemisphere of flame stretching beyond the farthest mountains, where life possibly is a rioting of
giants, and the skies, instead of showing a Christian
blue, are the color of a conflagration or of Hell itself!

In the moments of our greatest intoxication we are
joyously certain of being the first men in the world—
the first in order of time—the real Adams: Adams who
are to name all things, build all cities, found all king-
doms, be the prophets of all new religions, conquer,
fighting tooth and nail and body to body, the entire
world here below. Alone, innocent, unsophisticated,
pure, we feel we have the right to wipe out memories of
the past and the power to reweave reality on new looms
and in new patterns.

The world seems to us badly put together; life lacks

harmony and greatness; thought makes on us the impression of a gesture barely begun, of a punch checked in midair, of a black charcoal sketch that no one has yet filled in with color on the canvas.

There is much for us to do and much for us to do over again! Here we are—ready, waiting! Off with our jackets and hats! Farewell to our big books with their penciled margins, that gave us a thirst for knowledge but did not show us the way to the spring!

Here we are! Look at us! Strong fellows, eager for work, in our shirt sleeves, our hair blowing in the wind, picks and crowbars in hand, guns on our shoulders—masons and soldiers in one, like the Hebrews of Esdra. Oh, how the hammers ring! Oh, what a dust we are stirring up! Lime! Dirt! Rubbish! But . . . aha, there goes one old wall—see her fall! Boom! Bang! And a smoke hangs over us as on a good old-fashioned battlefield. And we sing and we shout back and forth as we destroy, and the shouts are shouts of war, and the songs songs of revolution!

There's no denying it: we are aflame with the military spirit. We would not don a regular's uniform for all the books in the world! But war is oxygen to our lungs. Every combat is to us a holiday. We think of our every word as a shot fired point blank at our enemy's heart. Every idea we have is a charge of TNT that never fails to dismantle a fortress! However, the regular army will have none of us! Our place is with the volunteers. We are guerrillas, brigands, rioters, disturbers of the peace, knights-errant looking for adventures of the sword as Casanova sought adventures of the skirt. Don Quixote is our patron, and only for his sake do we tolerate Sancho Panza; but we give vent to our feelings in a poisonous hatred of Sansone Carrasco, father and model of all philistines who are the sworn enemies of madness and all that resembles it.

We too are knights—gentlemen "of cloak and sword"—the sword for the shriveled hearts of the *patres conscripti,* the cloak for the shoulders of shivering, shuddering Dulcineas! Plumes on our hats, hands on our hilts, lowering glances to left and right— we are tough customers, I can tell you! What are you people doing around here? Better move along if you don't want to get stepped on! Cut your own throats before we cut them for you! Make way for *men!* For we must go forward! The weight of the world rests on our shoulders. We must attend to our job!

And, as we set about it, anything goes: a cuff here, a thrust there, just for practice! We too mistake windmills for giants! But we are not ashamed of the mistake. Are windmills not quite as dangerous? Try one yourself and you'll see that its arms are not less hard than the arms of Briareus!

Everything for nothing—everything or nothing! Have you a world you want discovered, a truth you want revealed, a tower or a wall to be torn down to the sound of our trumpets?

We are a nuisance to everybody; we drag God down from His throne in Heaven; we unseat kings from their thrones on earth. Not even the dead can rest in peace under the flowers and the lies on their graves, nor can chesty bronze celebrities, strutting on their pedestals of stone, be so sure of themselves!

We are bent on freeing ourselves of everything and of everybody. We insist on recovering a nudity of mind as nude as the nudity of the innocent Adam's body. Off with our coats—coats of religion! Off with our vests—vests of philosophy! Off with our shirts of prejudice, our neckties of idealism, our shoes of logic, our underdrawers of morality!

We must rub our skins clean, brush up our minds, disinfect our brains, take a cold plunge in running water, become children again, as innocent and natural as when we issued from our mothers' wombs. The dead must cease commanding the living. Books must no longer be the guides of life. Reason and History must drop their capital letters, resign their power, no longer keep us tied to school benches, waiting, our mouths open, our heads back, to be stuffed with bread-crumbs chewed in advance by others. Reason must be *our* Reason! History begins to-day! Year One of OUR era! *Incipit vita nova!*

A new heaven and a new earth! Scenery painted for the play in hand! Palaces run up over-night! Long façades, blazing with light, with a thousand windows and a flag at each one! Shouting and cheering along the streets! We must climb the heights, live on the mountaintops, look down upon the cities at our feet and be able to despise men at a distance!

Despise them and even hate and kill them! But at bottom love them! All we are doing is for them. We are talking just to dazzle and terrify them; for our real object is their deliverance: happiness for everybody! We are making war to improve them, we are shouting to arouse them, we are frightening them into a realization of their own needs. We have but one ambition at bottom: to be their masters, their leaders, their prophets—we would be happy to die, as Moses died, in sight of the vineyards of the Promised Land.

And since we are young and eager (and immune to writer's cramp), all these storms, all this revolting, all this boasting, results in four, eight, sixteen pages of printed paper—the weekly "journal of opinion"!

Tempestoso

"I am come to send fire on the earth."
LUKE.

Chapter 15: I Make a Speech at Night

THE review—the famous review, uppermost thought in
the mind of the man who would break his way into
the herd of the millions to awaken and enlighten
them; the long dreamed of and long promised review
with which he would take the world by storm, blud-
geoning the thick skulls of his contemporaries; the
journal so often proposed and so often planned which
would voice the aspirations of unknown geniuses, give
name and fame to anonymous grandeurs, reveal to the
masters of the present (to men no longer young, to men
of thirty and forty) that the real youngsters, the new
youngsters of twenty have also come of age and at last
acquired the right to speak; the magazine, the absolutely indispensable "organ," the sheet that fills a long-
felt want, a first delicious stretch for the muscles of
prisoners barely released from their chains, the first
joyous song of throats that have only murmured hitherto; the paper destined to be, intended to be, able
to be, the avenger of all despairs, the mouthpiece of
all angers, the club in every honest fist, the Wagnerian
trumpet blast of all defiance, the diary of all dreams,
the dynamite of all destructions too long postponed,
the rainbowed splashing of all daring thoughts—this
review, *the* review, our review, at last became a fact.

It took a deal of courage. We had no money. We

had no very definite idea about what we wanted to do, about whom and what we wanted to assail. There were few of us, and each with different opinions, ambitions, and temperaments. We did not know just where to begin. Yet the review became a fact.

We could not bring ourselves to wait for the air to clear. Our day had come. We had been talking of the thing so long! In our first cenaculum, a cheap restaurant, we passed whole mornings discussing a vehement, violent, incandescent magazine, to be called the *Flame* (*Vampa*) and devoted exclusively to masterpieces. All the mediocrities submitted to us, all the stupidities—whether articles for publication or books for review—we planned to burn publicly in an open square at the end of each week. We would tell what was what to everybody, laying down the law even (and especially) to the big fellows, to the celebrities. For our *gerente*—an editor to assume legal and personal responsibility for all we said—we would choose the ugliest and strongest brute we could lay our hands on, some scowling uncommunicative giant who would sign each number with his picture and not with his name.

Later on, with a different group of boys, we planned a paper of a high philosophical character, a journal of transcendental combat to be called *Becoming* (*Divenire*), with the divine words of Heraclitus, παντα ρει, for a motto. In the days when we had gone over to liberty—"liberty at all costs"—we began to talk of still another paper, which was to assail (sparing neither women nor children) myths, theories, religions, and individuals: *The Iconoclast*. On each of these occasions we polished up our weapons, poisoned our arrows, sharpened our teeth; but inevitably, for one reason or another—especially under pressure of our perennial persecutrix, Milady Poverty—we were forced to retire to cover, withdrawing into the darkness, the silence, and the discouragement of our dens.

But this time we were going through with the thing. Nothing would be able to stop us! Somehow or other we would get the necessary *lire* together, and as for the ideas . . .

We had even too many of them. However all that was needed was a strong hand on the tiller to keep the ship to its course. The other fellows, cowed by the "boss," would fall into line and follow all the more enthusiastically because they did not know where they were going.

And so it happened. I was the one to give a name, an idea, a manifesto, and the initial push to this little crowd.

It was Hallowe'en, and we were anxious to get started by the first of the year. We had no regular place of meeting during those early days and the cafés were too expensive; so every evening, just after sundown, we gathered in some *piazza* or other, thence proceeding, through the din and the lights of the city, to our conquest of principles and of men.

It rained almost every night. The city pavements were wet, muddy, full of puddles. But we did not notice. We made our way through the crowds, separated at times by passers-by or by wagons; then again, as disputes grew louder or as some new thought suddenly turned up in one of our brains, stopping, coming together, breast to breast, shoulder to shoulder, under the ruddy hesitant glare of a street lamp. We had no thought for the water through which we splashed, for the mud that spattered our clothes, for the jostling of hurrying people, for the persistent drizzle that soaked our hats or the frank rain that beat on our torn umbrellas. A mere nothing was sufficient to excite us, set us all afire: a title, a joke, an outline for some future article, a threat of a review announced menacingly against some famous name, a vague promise of an illustration or even of a subscription.

Every evening for two or three hours at a time we thrilled ourselves and each other with such dreams of words and paper. Nothing else in our lives was of any importance; everything was judged according as it bore or did not bear on the forthcoming magazine. We felt that the life of the city, of the nation, of the world, was revolving feverishly around us as its center, as impatient as we were, as anxious as we were, awaiting from us, a jabbering crowd of unknown enthusiasts, the burst of fiery light that would illumine everything, consume everything. How expect mankind to sit quiet while a revelation of new ideas and new geniuses, a destruction of old errors and old prophets, was about to shake the world?

In fact, new men came to join our group though

they did not know us. As our open conspiracy became common talk among the younger men, many of them hastened to join us, either out of curiosity or because of hankerings similar to ours. When we first talked of the paper we numbered only three or four; but now new faces kept appearing almost every evening, men we had never seen nor heard of. There were new hands to shake, new candidates to convert, new converts to fire with our zeal: bedraggled students, in black suits, their haggard eyes rimmed with purple rings from over-study; artists full of noise and poverty; timid striplings with not even down on their chins, who listened, astonished and thoughtful, to the big words and hair-raising plans of their elders; even maturer men, with brown or blond beards, who, after sterile years of waiting, felt the spell of this sudden gale of youth and madness. These newcomers had to be talked to almost in secret, one by one. They had to be tried out, tested, "placed"; then some bond of sympathy would develop with first one and then another; soon the intimate *tu* was generalized in a camaraderie which to-day made boon companions of strangers of yesterday.

All these forces had to be drawn together, consolidated, made compact and manageable for a concerted effort, ready to be hurled, united and irresistible, against an enemy unconscious of being such. I alone, among us all, had a fairly clear idea and plan, not to say also a certain gift for theoretical coördination. In me they all recognized the leader indispensable for the success of the now imminent enterprise. After a month or more of perambulating conference and confabulation in those stirring days of late autumn and early winter, I decided to prepare a great speech, or, if you wish, a great manifesto, to be read to those who had recently joined us, that they might say clearly, yes or no, whether we could count on their support even to a bitter end. Having, as I said, no headquarters of our own we had to fall back on the studio of one of our members—a painter, lately come from Rome, a youth of smiling well-contained enthusiasm. The studio, to tell the truth, was not really his. It had been "kindly placed at his disposal" by one of the Academies—the Academicians little suspecting what sort of company that young man was keeping! "So much the better," we said, "we will declare war on all Academies from within the very walls of an Academy!"

To avoid waking the custodians of that austere palace and arousing untoward suspicions we had to enter secretly. The meeting was called, if I remember correctly, for ten or eleven o'clock in the evening. We were admitted through a rear door opening on a dark alley, where one of our number was stationed on guard. As each of us, muffled in cape or overcoat, stole up out of the black fog of the night, he was made to tiptoe up a flight of long winding stairs, and then through a series of long corridors flanked by wooden walls, until he reached the sumptuous garret-studio that was to witness the solemn and formal foundation of a paper. A mysterious light—three or four candles stuck into the mouths of empty bottles or driven upon nails pro-

truding from the walls—suffused the great room which
was divided by huge beams sloping diagonally into the
corners. Half-finished canvases, decorative panels of
women dressed in red and of angels with silver trumpets in their hands, heroic designs of nudes and of
horses, languid faces of pre-Raphaelite beauties, surrounded us and stared at us with their eyes of white
lead. We took what seats we could find, chairs, empty
packing cases, tables, even places on the bare floor.
Within a quarter of an hour the studio was filled with
cigarette smoke and the hum of subdued voices.

But when I drew out the manuscript of my speech
absolute silence fell. And I began to read.

I cannot tell, at this late day, just what I said on
that night of mock conspiracy and joyous expectation.
There was a good deal of literature, much enthusiasm,
not a little rhetoric, numberless promises, tremendous
threats, and the effort, surely, to bring together and
formulate the ideas, intentions, sentiments, and virtues
of those young men who had so much faith in me and
in themselves. Among us there were painters who
hobnobbed with poets and poetry; men of letters
stuffed with criticism and history; wild-eyed philosophers, ever looking for quarrels to pick and enamored
of heights and depths; decorative pagans and impotent mystics; loafers and time wasters who had come
out of curiosity—a mob, in short, where disorganiza-
tion was the only system. And it was my task to
find the word, the slogan, the objective, the purpose,
that would touch each one and unite them all, sweep-

ing them into an irreparable commitment to our common "cause."

A name had to be found, a title, a symbol, which
would accommodate everybody, poets and philosophers,
painters and dreamers. It occurred to me that among
all the names sacred to our traditions, whether Florentine, Tuscan, or Italian, none was as appropriate as
that of *Leonardo*.

Leonardo, Leonardo da Vinci, better than the best,
had painted enigmatic portraits, flowers, rocks, and
skies; more scientific than the scientists, he had delved
into mechanics and anatomy, a patient searcher after
Truth; a greater writer than the writers, he had written
of life and of beauty in words of profound significance
and with imagery of surpassing elegance; he had
dreamed of the divine power of earthly man and—lover
of the impossible—of the conquest of the skies. The
vast thoughtful face of that old man who knew far too
much—his finely drawn lips, tightly closed under his
soft venerable beard—was before all our minds; and
his thoughts (which in those days had for the first time
become accessible even to the poorest) were in the
memories of many of us. In his name it was that we
consecrated our emergence from silence. Our paper
could be called *Leonardo,* and nothing else.

A new upflare of faith was kindled in me on that
eve of battle, as I stood there among those young men,
all tugging eagerly at the bit and ready for any adventure. And in that impassioned nocturnal harangue I
proclaimed our self-conscious, deliberate, and thor-

ough-going paganism as opposed to all the delinquency, cowardice, baseness, spinelessness of an age-old but rabbit-hearted Nazarenism. I proclaimed our fierce, hard-hearted individualism (or, as we said, *personalism*) as opposed to the solidaristic, collectivistic, socialistic insanity which was stultifying the spirit of youth, —leading young men to believe they were revolutionaries, whereas, in reality, they were sinking the vivid color of their own personalities in the mucky bog of a stupid, impotent, incompetent proletariate, or in the wretched low-down political life of a debased and humiliated Italy. And finally I proclaimed the uncompromising monopsychic idealism of the philosophers among us, who held that the external world did not exist, that reality was the shadow of a dream, that the universe was an unjointed fragment of our minds, that the old truths were lies put at the service of the brainless mob which saw certainty in contradiction, progress in destruction, and light in the absurd. Over this chaos, this clashing of tendencies, temperaments, actions, and reactions in us, I raised, as supreme ideal and common battle-flag, faith in unprejudiced intelligence, in the divine virtue of poetry, in the perennial miracle of art.

From time to time, raising my near-sighted eyes from the written pages and looking out into the play of dark shadows and reddish lights before me, I could see the attentive faces of my comrades, the disordered ranks of my regiment. In some of their eyes I thought I could recognize an eager, responsive yes. In my own ears I seemed to hear the excited palpitations of twenty, thirty hearts. A current of burning sympathy swept toward me, enfolding me in its warmth and stirring me so deeply that the last phrases, which, on a solitary winter's night at home, I had written out in my most flowing and harmonious style, came from my lips haltingly, smothered by a strange and unexpected emotion. Was I perhaps conscious that my life was beginning there, my real life as an apostle and an adventurer, there in that silent room, as I stood facing those men of the future, at that moment which was so full of solemnity for us all?

I do not know what my audience thought of my ringing tumultuous oration. But, at any rate, almost all of them, immediately afterwards, signed a large sheet of paper that a provident secretary had prepared and spread out on the table; and every one of them came and shook my hand. Our magazine was a going concern!

Each one promised a little money and much work.

Chapter 16: Palazzo Davanzati

A war tax of ten *lire* a month was imposed on each of us. Every one paid. There were the beginnings of a bureaucracy: a sort of secretary was appointed to assume the responsibility of giving body and substance to our dream. We went about in a crowd from printer to printer, looked upon with suspicion by directors and foremen, who could see we were innocent of experience and divine that we were poor. At last we succeeded in securing a room that was our very own—an editorial office!

How beautiful in those days the Palazzo Davanzati was, its lofty stone façade—the picture of age and nobility—fronting on the tumble-down ruins of the *Mercato Nuovo:* in the middle, a bombastic crown-topped coat of arms of the seventeenth century, jutting out, brown among its brown bosses; under the cornice, a fine loggia stretching across the upper story, open, airy, high up and free, Florentine, our very own, promising the passer-by, looking up to it from the street, a view of marble towers, of sun-bathed hills and serene skies. It was veritably the mansion of the old Florentine business man—money and all that money brings— solid, substantial, compact as the fortune he trusted to the banks of France and the Levant; dark, truculent as his partisan soul not yet weaned from factional strife; ample and spacious as the mind of a humanist and an esthete; sane as the art of the skilled and industrious craftsman he was. It may have been the influence of the name—but it reminded me somehow of the Davanzati translation of Tacitus, sober, stiff, but yet as meaty, as hearty, as full of nourishment, as the prose of our own Machiavelli!

But you should have seen the inside of the palace as it was in our time! Wretched lighting and no trace of broom or mop, rickety creaking stairways, walls scratched and bruised, the galleries half boarded in, and the great court, with its many twists and turns, littered with rubbish and junk and smelling of worse. In recent years they have cleaned it up, scraped the walls, repaired the interiors, in fact, turned it into a regular museum, with a catalogue, a man in livery at the door, and an admission fee of twenty-five cents! And you have to pay the twenty-five cents for the privilege of looking at all they have done: fresh paint, new tiling, oak furniture bought from the antiquarians, authentic paintings of great masters and the original Davanzati tapestries ransomed from the Jews! Everything now is neat, attractive, even comfortable, specially arranged for the benefit of foreigners, snobs, and people of money (and the education that comes with money) who want to know what a Florentine palace of the fifteenth century (as restored by a second-hand furniture dealer) looks like. But this is not the Davanzati Palace that we knew—filthy, leaky, all to pieces, but nevertheless full of a living life, inhabited by real men and not by costumes, statuettes, and medieval chests. It is, especially, not the Palazzo Davanzati that was the first home of a living, palpitating creation of ours, that shuddered at the tumult of our arguments, hissed with the clashing of our verbal swords, or echoed with the joyous songs and the mad laughter of our first invasion of the world.

We rented one of the rooms in the place from a corpulent and easy-going old man, who otherwise earned his livelihood by making cages for crickets and stringing fly screens for the doors of barber-shops. It was not a large room and nothing much could be said for the furnishings. We removed the bed that was in it, the lamp stand and the bureau, keeping the table, the rocker, and a number of plain chairs with broken legs. In a very few days we had transformed this bare and dilapidated "furnished room" to suit ourselves. The landlord, as if ashamed of the dirty walls, brought us a bunch of laurel which we distributed here and there along the moldings, with a big branch hanging from the ceiling. We ourselves brought photographs and prints of masterpieces of art, so that the nude women of Titian, the dignified old men of Leonardo, and dancing figures of mischievous fauns and conceited Apollos were soon lurking among the shiny foliage of green. Two rapiers hung from nails on one of the walls and on the door—for we had a private entrance all our own—there was a placard with the name of our divine protector in fine black letters—under it a red sun with rays squirming out in all directions like angry snakes. Every evening that bare wretched room was the scene of a celebration. Everybody came for two or three hours just to see what was going on, to start some argument, to tell some new story, to get some thrill or other. Anything was excuse enough for calling a general meeting. New recruits kept coming in, impatient and timid. My Giuliano was not in Italy at that time; but a letter from me giving him a lurid account of our preparations for the first issue, of my hopes for the future, of our advance announcement, brought him back home, posthaste, to join in the fray, where he immediately assumed a leading rôle.

Manuscripts began to arrive (corrections, cuts, refusals!); the first illustrations were patiently executed (little, hard, yellow pieces of box-wood into which the scoop cut furiously, sometimes slipping from the black guide lines); a printed notice was sent out, the first bulletin of war, booming with artillery and the clash of arms. What excitement when the first proofs arrived, still moist and on ugly paper, the ink not yet set, and full of blurs and ridiculous misprints, but for us divine messages of glory, our first strides toward men and immortality!

We had made up our minds that our review must be unlike any other in every respect—unusual even in its outward appearance. We used a dark, rough, handmade paper instead of smooth white. In place of ordinary engravings—the expressionless impersonal *cliché* and cold zinc—wood cuts made with our own hands! Figures and symbols in place of signatures! Poetical sonorous pseudonyms for our own unknown and discordant names! We all worked together in a feverish harmonious effort to make our first number beautiful, rich, original, startling in every detail. There was no division of labor: poets wrote on philosophy; philosophers became engravers; scholars tried their hands at lyrics; painters took up critique and theory.

Confusion, topsy-turvydom, all around us, every one working under tremendous nervous strain, as though we were starting the universe over again; as though humanity were awakening from centuries of sleep or rising from the ground after a thrashing by some god.

All the spirit of *Sturm und Drang* was with us as we stood there bending over proofs and drawings, screaming at the tops of our voices and with faces aflame over the problem of art, the genius of Michelangelo, the existence of matter. On our way out, down in the dirty courtyard, we started scuffles and fought sham duels just to work off the surplus energy generated by our tremendous excitement. Any weapons were in order: rapiers, canes, fists. Some of our bouts were in earnest and many a time we went home with knuckles bruised and faces scratched, but happy and glowing with the exercise, as though our bodies had a full right to share in the bubbling over of our spirits.

At last the suspense came to an end. After two months of talking, shouting, and working we went to press, and late one afternoon, shortly after seven o'clock, the first bundles of *Leonardo* were brought up the dark steps of the Palazzo Davanzati.

The day was the fourth of January, 1903.

Chapter 17: Vol. I, No. 1

THE review was all that we expected it to be. It *was* unlike anything else; and it led, like its authors, an irregular rambling life.

We began with eight pages, folio size, on hand-made paper and with designs, as I said, in wood cut. Issued every ten days, *Leonardo* dealt with everything more or less, including politics, but more especially with art than with philosophy; and what philosophy we had was such a lyrical, capricious, bizarre affair that it would hardly have been recognized as philosophy. After a few months, however, the artists and writers among us became less punctual about their dues and about their work. Some liked our sheet, others didn't (curiosity, enthusiasm, indulgence, pity—the whole gamut!), but it was widely read, especially among the younger men. On the other hand, we could not collect our money from the news-dealers, and advance subscriptions did not reach a hundred. By summer-time, as a result, only our two philosophers were left—Giuliano and I. But we stuck to our guns. We changed the format to review size, appearing less frequently, but with more pages and on any kind of shiny paper that we could secure. Art was sidetracked to a certain extent. Literature and politics were discarded entirely, and at last philosophy became mistress, queen, despot.

A philosophy of our own, I need not say; a philosophy which stood up proudly and caustically against the traditional philosophies of the hand-books, the professors, and the universities. We tried to revolutionize the very idea of philosophy—giving to thought, on the one hand, the freedom and fancifulness of poetry, and, on the other hand, to poetry—the poetry of the littérateurs (whom we detested)—a leaven, a ferment, an essence, of thought. Through us philosophy was to take on a new lease of life—a life quite in contrast to its past. Philosophy hitherto had always been rational: we set out to combat intellectualism with might and main. Philosophy had always been speculative and contemplative: we decided it should become something active, creative, taking its part in a necessary reformation of the world.

The first essential was to sweep the philosophy of the past—a philosophy of blind, spineless dullards—into the waste basket. It happened that the thought most in vogue in Italy at the time was Positivism; so we fell, like the wrath of Attila, on the Positivists. The barbaric and freedom-loving instincts of our earlier years came to life again in us: again we demolished, destroyed, dismembered, striking to right and left, sometimes with a perfect and a holy justice, then again, as our maturer judgment admitted, too precipitously, but always in good faith and in the name of a greater love. Such skirmishes and battles were the best part of every issue. We instituted periodical and regular massacres of nobodies and celebrities. We plotted exterminations *en masse,* and revolutionary *coups de main* on the Bastilles of the schools and universities.

Along with our work as housecleaners and policemen, we took some steps toward a reconstruction—outlines of new philosophies, discoveries, and expositions of new theories (mythical and Pindaric conceptions of the world); but especially platforms and programs, programs and platforms. We had so many ideas, and plan followed plan so swiftly, that we had no time to develop and expand them. Our mental adventures were so numerous that no sooner had we formulated the outline of one system or of one question for research than another would force itself to the front in our minds.

We were far from being destroyers, merely. We were the first, in Italy, to discuss many men, either our own or foreigners, forgotten or undiscovered, whom everybody is talking about to-day; though in those times even their names were unknown—and we spoke of them with reverence, love, and enthusiasm. We were among the first to stress and advertise certain modern ideas, certain tendencies, which others had failed to understand or even to detect, certain schools and movements to which no one in Italy had given any thought or attention before. We reawakened interest in the old mystics; we stirred (strangely!) one or two young men to an unexpected liking for mathematics; we raised and discussed problems that seemed at the time very remote from our national interests. Art served as a natural accessory to the piquant novelty of our quite unusual enthusiasm for ideas: engraved initial letters, cuts, and drawings, headings in colored ink, with running horses, sword hilts, sheaves of grain, giants with slings, knights with couched lances, were scattered over our pages like flowers tossed upon some parade of earnest reformers, like trumpet blasts of joy ringing above the tramp, tramp, tramp of heroic volunteers.

For some time after our first reorganization, Giuliano and I worked alone and most of our copies were distributed gratis. But soon other boys, a few at a time, joined us, attracted even from long distances to our work; and then veterans, serious mature men, sensed that there was both sincerity and depth in our bacchanalia of lyric idealism, in our ferocity as beardless conquistadores. They gave us money, they gave us books, they sent us articles.

On our long, broad, decorated pages, a strange and motley gathering appeared: acute mathematicians from Lombardy and colorful poets from Naples; philosophers of international renown; learned jurists adorned with all the majesty of the bar; aged scientists, precise, accurate, severe; and young students who were seeing their names in print for the first time. Our friends and subscribers increased in numbers; foreigners in far-away countries read and encouraged us; magazines both in Italy and abroad began to review us, often favorably, at other times in sharp reproof.

This was verily the heroic age of *Leonardo;* and it lasted some two years and a half. We had become a force to be reckoned with. All eyes were upon us. Every new issue, packed with ideas and resonant with fisticuffs, was eagerly awaited by a larger and larger audience. In some people surprise changed to enthusiasm, disdain to open hate; even women—most of them impassioned young girls—though they did not know us personally, turned to us with a sympathy that might easily have been taken for love.

Our review became the center and the organ of movements in thought; it was the starting point for new publications, collections, reprints; even to the plain readers of penny papers it began to stand for something coherent, constructive, and precise. We two, its founders and creators, were no longer alone and unknown. We began to prepare and publish the first books, large and small, which were to broaden and consolidate our influence. Other reviews asked us to write for them, and we got invitations to lecture here and there.

Our names, always mentioned together like the names of two brothers, had become familiar to all the new generation, and many young men turned to us as spiritual guides, as missionaries of an unbiased faith in Mind Regenerate. We lived in a perpetual state of excitement, of discovery, of activity of all kinds. Every day there was a new soul to discover, a new book to read, innumerable proofs to correct, a new battle to fight, unknown comrades to answer, and new friendships to deepen.

It was a real life that we now lived, a life of surprises, of pitfalls, of creation, formation, expansion, ascension. But its very intensity and success wore us out. After two years Giuliano, my one companion, my true comrade, left me for other ties, for other scenes. I went on alone. Others came to me to help. New currents of thought flowed through the review.

But these new colleagues, these latest arrivals, did not have the ardor—or the unselfish devotion of the first. Other dreams—more dangerous ones—laid hold on my mind and clouded my judgment. I skirted the dark seas of magic. I thought I could discern in various ancient superstitions and disguised esotericisms the first steps leading to Divinity. My idealism became mysticism, my mysticism occultism; and occultism might have led me to theosophy, had I not stopped in time.

Gradually I let up in my work. My impetuousness died down. The interest others had been taking in me weakened. Once remarkable for its rich and animated variety, *Leonardo* now became merely interesting. It lost its outward charm. It had fewer pages. The illustrations were discontinued, and literature reappeared. It was just a review, in short. My mind, always astray among boundless ambitions, in comparison with which a bit of printed paper seemed an insignificant ridiculous thing, wandered from my task. Internal dissensions and external estrangements hastened the end. For five years I had been there exploding, cursing, dreaming—before others, for others. It could no longer satisfy me. The effort required was too great; and at the same time the results to be achieved seemed pitiably small. Besides, the mind cannot go on outflowing forever. It demands repose, leisure to renew, to refertilize itself after so many seasons of blossoming and harvesting. I felt the need of a new period of meditation and reflection, of a new plunge into solitude.

After five mad years of struggling, battling, searching, and striving, I deliberately killed the child of my dreams, a child dearer to me than my very self. It was mid-summer, the month of August. The cover of the last issue was blood red, on it a sheaf of gory arrows. Yet it had an air of sadness, dejection, discouragement—like a bier for a murdered love.

Chapter 18: Flight from Reality

Too many memories, too many regrets for lost things! All this warmth and color of the past, all these external facts and vicissitudes—what do they amount to? Poetry, literature—vanity! What matters here is the story of a soul, the story of my soul, not the story of a palace or of a magazine. I should not fall into such weaknesses, and if shame has not erased all traces of them from my book it is because they too are symptoms and proofs of a pathetic and sentimental element in my character which I am unable to repress even during my most violent orgies in logic and philosophy.

Can it be that I shall ever prove unable to see idea without body and shadow, ever unable to understand a system of thought save through its manifestations as life, as daily experience of senses and emotion? Bark, husk, vesture, mask, these are—that I know, that even I know too well—nothing but bark, husk, vesture, mask! They are nothing more—nothing more substantial, more intimate, more essential—than that. And bark drops off, garments wear out, masks lose their color; and what is left is concept, the inner indestructible skeleton of Truth. And this covering is accidental, contingent, variable, transitory. Manifestations for the mere convenience of others, vehicles through which these spiritual messages are transmitted,

I felt them so close to me that they seemed to be all mine and so alive in spirit that I never thought of them as dead. If, by chance, I remembered that their bodies were nothing but ashes, dust, that their voices were stilled forever, I grieved at having lost them too soon, at having been born in an age too late to know them. Never have I felt such dislike of death as at those moments. Never have I loved any warm living being as I loved those dead—cold corpses buried under monuments and centuries. At times it seemed as though they actually were with me in my room; or that I met them on streets that I liked better than other streets; or on the banks of roaring rivers, or by crumbling walls; and many a time I tried to talk to them, to tell them of my great love and my loneliness. But they would look at me in silence, without moving. If I tried to step nearer, they would vanish.

The books in which I first became familiar with their thoughts, their loves, their hates, I remember in their shapes, their colors, their styles of type, even in the spots and creases of their pages; and I shall never forget them. Playthings? Sentimental trinkets of loves that have passed? Far more than that! Sacred relics, real relics, these mementos of my best life— dirty, cheap volumes full of misprints and wretchedly executed; editions printed wholesale at a cent or two a copy; books bought secondhand, covered with ink-spots and pencil-marks, their pages torn and dog-eared; heavy tomes bound in leather and kept apart by themselves like holy things.

words, spoken words, written words, pages with print
and pictures; sheets of paper published from time
to time; sheets of paper bound in pamphlets, books,
volumes—all these are but experiments, gropings,
glimpses, murmurings, languages in formation, beginnings of speech, which few understand and nobody
cares to study. Every one of us who has a real life
of his own—by that I mean an individual, personal,
intimate life of sense and thought—is an Adam who
must name all things over again for himself and con-
struct a new vocabulary and a new language of his
own. In his mouth the words of his fathers have a
different savor, a different sound, a different meaning.
He may speak of light, but his mind may be thinking
darkness. Let him utter the most commonplace word
—"man" for instance! And he will be seeing a man
of his own, a man who, you may rest assured, in no
way resembles that man on the corner, or that man
at the window, or Plato's man, or God's man; but is
his own man—his ideal, his type, his dream, his model
of a man!

And each of us must recomprehend this inner Self
of his, when it has passed over to the dead forever,
with all the other dead, all the Selves he daily kills with
the slow poison of oblivion. And when he would speak
of that dead Self, he must reconstruct it in terms of
the dictionary it used, in terms of its grammar, of its
mental syntax. Fruitless indeed it would be to pick
over the rags that were its gala attire or to repeat the
epigrams it wrote to stabilize (to immobilize—to kill,

that is) its intuitions and its fleeting mastery of the fleeting Eternal! Body and matter are not enough. We are looking for the spirit, for the thing that lies deepest down. If painting is impossible—well, try geometry! I am not going to give you a sentimental solo about myself. Must you have anatomy? Here is my body: take it, flay it, cut it up, dissect it! This is my body, this is my flesh—but where is the breath that gave it life, where the idea that gave it being? In this dust-heap of memories? Among this rubbish that strews the bottoms of these drawers? Among these papers spotted with the mold of almost ten years? Pray, spare your pains! I am not there! I alone can lay my hand on the central knot that binds, unites, unifies this tangled mass of the writings, proclamations, attacks, defenses, of a noisy apostle and propagandist. Now the period of Storm and Stress has passed (history, anecdote, human interest!); but the real source of all the noise, of all the tempest, lies in the Self that remains, in the undying and absolute Ego which has contact with the Eternal and *must* partake of the Eternal.

This central knot of all my thinking of those days was a *flight from Reality*—non-acceptance, rejection, banishment of reality. A radical, deep-reaching Pessimism had ceased to be the ultimate and only basis of my conception of the world; and I no longer thought of proposing voluntary universal suicide by poison to a terrified humanity. But cosmic despair, though it had lost ground in me as theory, had become a permanent state of mind in me and lingered as an ineradicable taint in my blood and in my soul. I no longer gave it explicit formulation, but it suffused every act of my brain. "No thought is born in me that does not bear the image of death," wrote the aged Michelangelo; no thought on things was born in me that did not smack of bitterness and scorn. Young men, people say, are embodiments of hopeful confidence. That is not true, at least not true of us all. For when a youth (if he be not irreparably a pig) steps forward to take possession of life, he is so filled with splendid hopes and aspirations, so certain of his near-sublimity, of his all but divine capacities, that he cannot fail to be continuously slapped in the face by the disillusionment which life and reality bring. He has hoped for a flowering Paradise and he finds himself in a most putrid Hell. He thought to find brothers with hands outstretched and meets instead a pack of ravenous snarling beasts, ready to rush at him and tear him to pieces. He pictured life as faultless marble, granite of even grain, out of which he could hew his own image with the hard chisel of will; and instead he finds a lump of mucky dung in his hands which either cannot be molded, or which, molded indeed, will not hang together.

Too much idealism, say the wiseacres who have gotten used to the smell. And "too much" is right! Young men die of that "too much" more often than of the little piece of lead they shoot through their hearts. But verily I say unto you: there is no surer sign of "smallness" of nature than contentment with everything. Peace can come only when youth is over, when the cycle of inner and outer experience has been completed, when we find solace for the eternal nothingness of things in exquisite enjoyment of the Now that will never return again.

So, at that time, I felt a violent dislike for the Real. I did not approve of the universe as it was and I did not accept it. Like a Capaneus stuck in an earthly Inferno, I drew up proud and scornful. I was inclined to deny reality and all imitations of Reality, to hold the laws of real life in contempt, and create a different and more perfect Reality of my own.

What, in fact, was that spirit of infuriated anarchy I felt—my brazen disrespect of men and dogmas—if not a reaction against the past, against everything fixed, disciplined, established, regular? What was my love for everything crazy and absurd except a revulsion from the commonplace, from the ordinary, from the safe and sane? Why such contempt for rules of conduct and good manners, for popular idols, for prudent counsel, for all the so-called "bourgeois virtue," if I were not sick of the accursed fact that never changed, sick of wisdom, sick of "obligations," sick of "sure things" and the worship they inspire?

I attacked Positivism because the Positivists pretended to be nothing but registrars of a reality duly witnessed and attested under their hands and seals. I swallowed idealism whole, even in its extremes, because its transference of everything to the mind, its calling the very existence of matter into question, gave it a strong seasoning of extravagance and paradox. It was my loathing for the present that drove me back to the past, to solitary communion with a few of the great dead. It was loathing for all existing things that set me to dreaming. It was loathing for men that led me out into the rural silences to seek friendships with the trees and flowers. My favorite word in those days was: freedom—freedom from this and from that, from the Now and from the Hereafter, from the Here and from the There—freedom from everything.

I wanted to strip the clothes from myself and from others, to return to complete nudity, to the terrifying freedom of the absolute universal atheist. And when I thought I had rid myself of all kinds of trumpery, that I had thrown off the ordinary cares and concerns of other mortals, then I decided to build a world of my own—and in two ways: by power of mind, and by activity of imagination—through will and through poetry.

My much-talked-of "pragmatism" of those days did not indeed concern me so much as a rule of research, as a test of procedure, as a tool of method. I was look-ing farther ahead. At that time a thaumaturgic aspi-ration was much on my mind—a need, a desire so to purify and strengthen my spirit as to enable it to act on things without recourse to instruments and media, thus eventually achieving omnipotence and the power of working miracles. So I did not stop at the "will to believe." I went on to the "will to do"—to the "possibility of doing." If only my will could extend its scope from my body to the things around me—so that the whole world would be its body, obedient to its every command, just as these few muscles of mine are obedient to it now! I pretended to start from a logical precept (pragmatism); but in my secret heart I was jealous of Divinity and eager to become a rival of Divinity!

A similar feeling led me toward art. I had no patience with "literature": all that was false, elegant, fictitious, factitious, decorative, as implied in that word, repelled me. And though I loved some of the old poets with all my heart I had an unconquerable dislike for people who wrote poetry, short stories and novels for the amusement of others and for gain.

Philosophy seemed to me much higher and nobler than art, but philosophy itself led me back to art. To express certain of my thoughts with greater force and warmth I began to make inordinate use of imagery. I tried the myth as a form of exposition; from the myth I developed the legend; then I wrote dialogues and "visions"; and little by little I admitted conversations between "types" taken from poetry and tradition, which soon began to live on their own account, speak a different language, and take a hand in new adventures. Thus I passed almost unconsciously from a purely lyric self-expression to what was virtually the tale or the short story; and the idea which had been my goal, my all, was merely part of the raw material for my imagination to work with. The panting restless churning of thoughts in my brain, the bitterness of my disillusionment, the impetuousness of my apostleship, seemed to find more adequate and powerful expression in these poetic creations of ambiguous form. So, quite apart from any intention of mine, a world of phantasy grew up about me in opposition to the real world, and into it I could withdraw to weep and live in my memories. In it I was master and king above all law. That is where, in those days, I met my modern Devil; listened to the confessions of my "sick gentleman" and my "Queen of Thule"; harkened to the groans of the unhappy Hamlet and the confidences of Giovanni Buttadeo and Don Juan Tenorio. They came forward to meet me out of the shadows of the Unreal; yet they seemed to me more alive than the living that scuffled along the pavements at my side; and only in their company did I feel that I could understand and be understood, love and be loved. A troubled, cloudy, murky world it was, where darkness overmastered light and the tragedy was the commonplace; a world that was inhabited by youths pale and disillusioned, and men possessed of fixed ideas and tortured by wild fears; a world where actions were few and far between, but thoughts tempestuous; where the plausible blended with the fantastic and life with death. It was another world. It was my world: a world of darkness and terror, yes, but at least not this world, the world where everybody lives!

So while I was trying to subjugate the real and refashion it through the miracles of a sublimated Will,

I was actually creating a provisory substitute, reality peopled by the docile specters of my Fancy. Poetry is a ladder leading to divinity—to labor in art is itself a beginning of creation. Poet and prophet to-day— and to-morrow, perhaps—God!

Chapter 19: My Dead Brothers

I DID not accept reality.

These are the most temperate words I can find to express my nausea at the physical, human, rational world that shut me in, denying me air to breathe and space to flap my restless wings. Yet they are not the exact words I should wish. They do not say everything, they do not make everything clear. I did not accept *that* reality; but only because I wanted another—a purer, more perfect, more angelic, more divine reality; and I did my best to see the spiritual harmonious world I looked forward to come into being, as the statue, which the artist has seen in his mind and willed to be, springs from a rough block of marble freshly quarried from the mountain side. I did not accept an ordinary, superficial reality because I sought a better, truer, profounder one. I denied the past, I denied the present to fix my gaze, my aim, my heart's desire, on a grander miraculous future.

And even with this I have not said everything: I have within me a feeling somewhat akin to remorse; and I am unable to suppress it. I deny the past—but is it not to the past that those great souls belong, those brothers of mine—dead and buried in their tombs but still so alive and present to me, who consoled me during the years of my solitude, during the years of my exodus to the Promised Land? They are the ones who showed me the path to freedom and gave me the thoughts, the figures, the words, which best express my real self. Be I great or small, it is they who made me what I have been, what I am! They gave me comradeship during sleepless nights, refreshment during periods of repose, encouragement and inspiration in combat—the guardian angels of my best days! To them, to them alone, I owe that contempt for mediocrity, that anxiety for perfection, which ever leaves me a sort of heroic dissatisfaction with myself. They first pushed me toward the heights, giving me a ladder for escape, weapons for revolt, tools for destruction, and my very vision of a celestial universe, of a beatitude without burdens and without baseness. How could I deny them without repudiating myself and all that was best in me?

And them, indeed, I did accept. Accept? I sought them out with more love than a son has for a loving father, with more admiring tenderness than a boy feels for his big brother. These dead and my hills! These dead and my trees! These dead and my ravenous hungry spirit! Ah—I contradict myself? Not in the least! That part of my past which they constitute (those men, those dead, those teachers, friends, allies of mine) gave me my scorn for all the rest—gave me the courage and the intelligence to obtain my freedom. Indeed I accepted just enough of the past to make the rest hateful to me. I loved them because they incited me to this hatred. I sought them out because they aided me in my escape.

But what need have I of such excuses? These I have been making are, to tell the real truth, after-thoughts, posthumous quibblings to explain a sympathy that was spontaneous and ever fresh. I was happy with them, and with them only. I saw the world through their far-seeing eyes. I thought in the directions their thought suggested. They were as necessary to me as bread, as water, as sky, as all pure, good, wholesome things that cost nothing and without which one cannot live. I loved them more than any one could ever love a woman, for a woman has but one face and one soul, while they gave me ten souls, a thousand souls, a soul for joy and a soul for sorrow, a soul for sublation and a soul for sanctification. I loved them passionately, madly, immoderately. Have I not said that I always sought for greatness; that I—small, despicable, crazy as I may have been—was always determined to be great, to make myself great? Only with them, with their genius, with their greatness, could I be sure always to find and feel the panting urge which impelled me ever toward the heights far above the bestial mob of the plains. They gave me that *panem solum* by which I could live. They gave me courage to trust my native instincts. They spurred me on when my strength failed. Their dead eyes smiled at me from the frames around their pictures, when I grasped my pen between my lean fleshless fingers and forced it across the paper in my rambling handwriting to spin the thread of an idea or expand a dialogue between my phantoms.

And I remember the very places, the very moments in which I absorbed them into my being, in which I felt them closest to me—mine—radiant before my eyes in a brilliant, penetrating light. Dante! Dante I associate with summer dawns, a cold stone bench high up above the city, the soft splashing of a near-by fountain in a pool of muddy water. Shakespeare I read for the first time by candle light on winter nights in my chilly, uncomfortable room. I first felt Baudelaire on days of autumn, when the leaves were dropping from the trees along the deserted drives of the *Cascine,* and the silver Arno was turning crimson for the festival of sunset. Shelley means spring to me—a path leading through a grove of acacias and ash trees, where I sang aloud the most anguished invectives of Prometheus. Taine carries me back to the great reading-room of the library,—cold light filtering through dust-covered skylights, across which from time to time white pigeons flew. I probed the *Unicum* of Stirner on the brick wall of grassy hallowed ground by the side of a church, where a faint odor of incense still lingered—a hilltop, cool breezes, a large shady elm. I declaimed the verses of *Zarathustra* behind a stone shelter which I had thrown up against the wind near a shepherd's hut on the lonely pasture lands of Pratomagno summit.

But these were not the only companions of my secluded vigils at home, of my thoughtful walks and delicious hours of repose among living things under open skies. I forget no one of you—you, the true loves of my teens and early twenties. One by one you

My immediate object was a simple one: to increase the power of my will until it became a limitless will, until my spirit could command men and things without recourse to external instruments, until, in other words, I could do *miracles*—nothing more, nothing less!

The saints and the magicians (or people who were perhaps a little of both: the Hebrew prophets and the Indian fakirs) pretended they had performed miracles —the ones without trying, almost without wishing, to; the others by subjecting themselves to severe régimes of life, sustained by secret doctrines and forces beyond themselves. But at any rate miracles there had been! Already the rudiments of an art of miracles existed! Mere beginnings, mere hints, mere rudiments—but enough for a beginning. The problem was to reconstitute the art as a whole, rediscover its basic rules and learn how to apply them. Even if the miracles which the biographers of the saints and the theorists of magic told were not true miracles in the strict philosophical sense of the term, that would make no difference to me. All the better even: they were facts out of the ordinary; examples of unusual faculties; striking manifestations of the power of will, cases of men blessed with divine endowments. That much would do!

By studying these men, going deep down into their lives, observing the methods they used to do what they did, I would in the end be able to discover their secrets—the basic process common to all miracles.

pass before my memory recalling—with a clutch at my heart—a date, a view, a verse, a thought. I have a debt to pay to all of you, a debt which I am paying as I go on through life trying to pass on to others a spark, perhaps, of the fire you kindled and kept aflame in me.

And to you, the poets, I owe the deepest debt! For it was you who took me up, like Satan, to a mountain top and whispered in my ear: "Behold! All this wealth, this youth, this beauty is yours, can you but see and understand it!" To you, Dante—father Dante!—I owe a fierce longing for Paradise and my coarse, vulgar, violent explosions of noble scorn! To you, Leopardi—my brother Leopardi—exquisite enjoyment of ineluctable despair, and a clear pitiless vision of the ridiculous infamies of man; to you, Shelley, heart of hearts (drowned like a god in *mare meum*), the pathetic vivification of nature, the love of sumptuous refinements in a gilded world and pity for defeated giants; to you, Baudelaire, fraternal spirit, a perverse and unconquerable delight in cursing, a passion for the bottomless pits of carnal existence from which there is no escape and over which there is no heaven, and an ecstatic transfiguring of everyday pettiness and baseness; to you, Heine, the shrill laughter that conceals sadness, zest for disemboweling the puppets of the mythologies; to you, Walt Whitman, friend of my early childhood, the sweeping breath of the sea, of the multitudes, of the life of men, a warm and generous embrace of all beings and all peoples; to you, Carducci, poet of my Tuscany's marsh-lands, the furies of a restless lion, a love of cold gales from the north, of uncompromising revolutions, of pugnacious Dianas, and of Italy's greatness.

Can I tell what I owe to Shakespeare, what I owe to Goethe? Were they poets merely, authors of dramas, tragedies, mysteries? Did they not show me worlds that have never been described in books, lead me on to vaster scenes, introduce me to ideas made flesh, let me eavesdrop on the dialogues of heroes, see the wonders of Blessed Isles? Did I not learn from them that life is a dream and the dream reality, that the most profound, the most terrifying, the most illumi-nating thoughts are not to be found in the volumes of the philosophers? Did I not talk more than once with the pale Hamlet? Did I not go seeking the real life with Doctor Faust? Were they not both living familiar parts of my being?

In my mind Shakespeare and Goethe joined Don Quixote and the Idiot, sometimes Julien Sorel and Peer Gynt, and often Doctor Teufelsdroeck consorting with Didimo Chierico and Filippo Ottonieri. It is they who made me, who still sustain me, and govern me. From Cervantes I took the sacred madness of the ideal and scorn for the vulgar sanity of the Sancho Panzas; from Dostoievski the sacred madness of love for the unfortunate and the tremendous fascination of inner tragedies of the soul; from Stendhal the stoicism of the man who without flinching can see things of this world as they are, and an inclination for secretiveness

born of modesty; from Ibsen self-respect, self-knowl-
edge, self-defense; from Carlyle, the discovery of spirit
under symbol and vesture, of the everlasting "Yea" in
the everlasting "Nay"; from my two Italian brothers
that melancholy pensive shrewdness which understands
but can hardly restrain its tears.

But why do I not mention—and before all others—
Edgar Allan Poe? It was he who introduced me to the
complexities of terror. And Novalis? For it was he
who won me with a mystic belief in power. And what
of the philosophers? Plato: handsome boys, shrewd
old men, myths, sophisms, banquets, and porticos
along a seashore. Berkeley: Hylas and Philonous,
spending the foggy hours of a London dawn in a park,
demolishing matter and universals. Schopenhauer: discovery of thought and pain, of will and renunciation.
Nietzsche: sunshine, destruction, noble mountains,
snow-capped, and the laughing dance of genius set free.
Stirner: dialectic anarchy, hideous solitude, an eloquent gospel of egoism, an extremist rebellion of the
timid man. But among the thinkers I loved more than
all others the wreckers of moralities, those who knew
what men are like and were not afraid to say so;
heroic but resigned despairers, cynics who scrape the
paint off the frescos of idealism and disclose the holes
in the plaster underneath, who cut into silver plating
that the cheap lead it hides may be paid for at its
real worth; severe, courageous logicians; men without
ideals; the intellectual customs guards and quaran-
tiners of humanity. Especially the French! The

rhythmic flow of Montaigne's wisdom; the volcanic eruptions of Diderot; the clear and vivacious systematizing of Taine; even the gay witty skepticism of Voltaire; the moral polytheism of Brewster, and the naturalistic cynicism of Remy de Gourmont.

This was my world, my real country, my real fraternity. This divine city of my soul had for background the mountains of Leonardo; for monuments, the heroes of Michelangelo—sad even in victory; for pictures, the lights and shades of Rembrandt. From time to time the solemn cadences of Bach's sonatas, the more passionate movements of Beethoven's symphonies, the heroic motifs of Wagner's choruses, broke the silences. Only among such thoughts, such images, such sounds, did I feel that the world was worthy of me.

Chapter 20: Small Remainders

BUT stronger than my love for the great dead was my scorn for the small-fry living—for all of them, for those I knew and for those I had never seen; for those who belittled me and those who applauded me; for those who welcomed me and those who snubbed me.

With the exception of three or four of my companions who shared my hatreds and adventures, I did not consider any living man my equal. No man seemed worthy of judging me, or even of standing at my side. I seriously believed that I was the only living being without prejudices, without blinders for my eyes, without sham, without nonsense, without stupidities inside my head—the only one capable of routing hypocrisies and exposing frauds; of ridding Valhalla of old gods and modern fools; of stripping off the finery that a prostituted habit and convention paraded in public; of liberating humanity from the humiliating mental servitude that shackled it. My purpose was to free (the word I used to myself was "help") the very ones whom I scorned. I scorned them because they were not free; and because they so richly deserved my scorn, I was anxious to free them. I wanted to raise them to my level, not stoop to theirs. It was to make men of them that I told them they were beasts; it was to prove my love of them that I used the lash. If I descended

143

to their plane in so doing, it was only the better to enjoy lashing them. I wanted to make them worthy of
me, worthy of the ideal type of humanity which I represented—a humanity wholly free, wholly spiritualized,
immune to the taint of any faith. Savage master that
I was, I did not try to coddle my pupils with music and
blandishments. My method was to wake them up,
shake them up, set them moving! At that time I
might have taken Petrarch's verse as the motto of my
life:

"Io venni sol per isvegliare altrui."

I came to arouse people, yes; but arouse them not by
coaxing them, tickling them, but by using a club on
their backs, gripping them by the front of their coats,
and slamming them back against a wall that their
shame and anger at such insulting treatment might
force them to a show of gumption, an act of real man-
hood. I behaved toward men much as animal trainers
go at their lazy sleeping lions in a menagerie. I jabbed
them in the ribs, I burned them with hot irons; I gave
them ferocious cuts with the whip—jabbed them with
the most bitterly sarcastic thrusts I could find; burned
them with hard cruel epithets and pitilessly sincere ac-
cusations; whipped them with sneers at the meanness
of their lives, the insignificance of their ideals, the
primitiveness of their ideas, their ignorance of everything, and their incapacity for deep understanding and
sound reasoning.

No one was safe from my sudden and rapid offensives. If there was no question up for discussion I brought one up on purpose, starting an argument on my own territory, involving my opponent in difficulties of my own making and raining merciless blows upon him. If there was a real issue I would turn it and twist it in such a manner that I alone was left on the battlefield brandishing syllogisms and hurling vituperation to right and left. If some timid individual appeared, I would force him to say something and then I would ridicule him for its absurdity. If I met a garrulous talker I found indescribable delight in humbling his assurance and reducing him to silence. If an unpleasant truth could be told to anybody I was always the first to come out with it without evasion or circumlocution. If I was aware of a defect, a shortcoming, a weakness in any one, I soon found a way to take advantage of it for a pointed thrust or a formal indictment. When my friends wanted to rid themselves of a bore, a timekiller, a pedant, a fool, they left the matter to me; and exceptional indeed the case where he did not disappear once and for all in confusion and humiliation. I had but to find the hidden canker in a man's soul to make it eventually the subject of remark, bluntly accusing him of it *coram populo*. And no sooner had I sensed the most vulnerable and painful point in some person's inner life than I touched on that point and focused attention upon it. A random unguarded phrase and I was capable of drawing the most unexpected conclusions from it, developing its implications, showing its remote bearings on character; and I would hammer and beat upon them until my poor victim begged for mercy or took to his heels. A few spoken words sufficed me to analyze the psychology of almost any man, and when I had taken it to pieces I would put it together again and set it down with a thump in front of him that he might see himself as others saw him and blush for shame.

Everything served my purposes in this daily warfare of sniping and sharpshooting against mankind: learned quotations, new ideas, names of unknown "authorities," arguments *ad hominem*, dialectic quibbles, literalisms in handling words; contradictions caught on the wing; banter, wit, violence of manner, jest, ridicule, glances of commiseration, guffaws, grins, insults. Anything went! All was fair! If only I could make these idiots see the superiority of my mind and of my view of things! When my victims did not come to me I went to them to smoke them out of their retirement. Having cleaned up one neighborhood, I would go looking for new people, to enjoy a fresh choice and a greater variety of despicable souls.

In a short time I acquired the reputation of being either a "terror" or an intolerable boor; and I was flattered by both judgments. For some people I was an ill-mannered snob; for others an apostle of frankness; for some I was a disagreeable rascal; for others a hero of sincerity. Many, the majority even, shunned me as they would the plague; others, of stronger metal, stood the strain, sought my company, and eventually forced my friendship. This method of dealing with men was not alone the necessary outlet of my belligerent rough-knuckled character, nor even merely the natural counterpart of my boundless pride and conceit: it was also a method of trying men out, a touchstone for finding the best and the strongest. Those who took offense at my words did me a favor by going away. Others hated me; and this too was a gratification, for I have always felt a greater need of enemies than of friends. Some valued me the more highly. Fascinated by my very violence, they took their medicine in good part because they realized that more often than not I spoke the truth, and that the truth thus brutally stated was of far more benefit to my victims than it was to my progress in this world. I made some friends by sheer dint of drubbing and roughing them. Keener than the rest, these few were able to see the affection hidden under my scorn. They knew that behind my shield with its Gorgon's head a poor sentimental poet was shivering with far more capacity for friendship than the smooth-tongued, perfectly mannered youths of society.

All the more so since I did not always use my bludgeon on the people about me. I liked, for instance, to stir them up with sudden questions as serious, as fundamental as they were unexpected, questions such as are never put to people and which may even seem absurd and useless, questions which men hardly dare to ask themselves, and yet which involve their whole understanding of the world, all values, and all life. I was bent on forcing others to think, to reflect, to examine into themselves, into their souls, their futures, their ideals. I wanted to turn their gaze inward upon depths which they shrank from penetrating, to bring them face to face with their inner selves, to see themselves as they really were, in order then to change their minds, to turn in some other direction, to quicken their pace, in order, at any rate, not to forget—if they were still in time—to change. Many men owe their first awakening to me, or else crises of terrible dejection from which they finally emerged as real men, though returning to the pathways they had previously chosen. In this world of heavy and eternal sleepers some one must have the courage to shout, "Who goes there?" every now and then and to sound reveille at an earlier hour than usual. There must be some one to wipe the rouge from people's cheeks that they may have one good honest view of their real freckles. If then they haven't the courage to see themselves as they are, let them return to their deception again. Let them pose as honest men though they be only rascals. Let them pose as geniuses though they are only fools! That is no concern of mine! I have done my duty!

So hate me then, and curse me! Look the other way when I go by. Men are not born again of poultices and homeopathy. It takes strong and radical treatment. You must cut where there is cutting to do; cauterize where the gangrene has started. We must rout out of their quilts and blankets those who have never known the fresh fury of the wind or the healthy sting of driving snow save through the window panes of comfortable houses. If you can't stand fresh air—so much the worse for you and so much the better for the undertaker!

I in no way regret my frankness and belligerency in the past. I cannot help without hurting. I cannot love without despising.

Chapter 21: And Not a Word of Love?

I HAVE passed my twentieth year. Youth is now overflowing into its full vigor. Real life has begun, life in closer contact with a concrete humanity. No longer sufficient unto itself, it serves notice of intention to spill over and spread out upon others—upon everybody. And of love—not a word? How can that be?

The age of twenty is the classic springtime of romantic idylls that makes even the hardest hearts swell with life and burst into blossom. It is the pagan summer of the senses, the Herculean July of uncontrolled desire, when in every glance lurks a longing for pleasure, when every hand seeks a beautiful body to caress, when kisses burn like fever on lips that will not, cannot, be torn apart. It is the season of love in the short year of life. At this period woman (in long braids and in short skirts borrowed from her cousin or powdering her face at the dresser of a maiden aunt) enters the life of a man, and plants in his flesh or in his heart memories that will outlast all others. From then on a man is no longer alone; he no longer belongs entirely to himself: this woman, virgin or prostitute—it matters little—begins to possess him and make him over.

Is this not the moment for confidences—confessions about timid affections, sentimental sorrows, consuming passions? Of love, not a word?

No, my lady! (Of course, no one but a woman would think of asking such a question.) No, signora! I can give you no hope! Love will not be mentioned either here or later on. If you have begun to read this story of a man's life with the indiscreet hope of meeting a woman sooner or later, throw it aside right now and think no more about it. I will not write of love, nor will I introduce women of any kind.

If this is a novel, it will be a novel without love. If it is history, it will be history without women. Dull perhaps, incomplete I dare say, unconvincing doubtless! As you will, my sweet lady, but so it shall be, so it must be; because *I* will it so—I who am master of my life, my soul, the things I do.

Oh, dear lady, it is not that love has not played its part in my life. On the contrary! Love, I mean too, in all the senses of that word: platonic love, love of the bull-pens, spiritual love, physical love, sentimental love, sensual love.

There have been women in my life. "Women," the plural of "woman"! I don't say many, please don't misunderstand! I was not a Don Juan—I couldn't be! But there were women, real women, women of flesh and blood—and nerves; women like the women we admire in the great novels and hope sometime to own in real life.

So then, women!

Girls, enthusiastic and over-ardent, simple and wholesome girls, without a trace, a spot, of literature; and—alas!—married women, intelligent, cultured, devoted, free; and again—I am not ashamed to confess it—harlots—melancholy women these, who carried on their trade more honestly than many others. Some of them were beautiful; some were pretty; some were attractive; some were interesting. I loved them all, one after another, loved them with soul and body, or soul alone, or body alone. I was the ingenuous lover and the bold lover, the tender lover and the jealous lover, the noble lover and the mean lover—as all men are with all women. I have made my bold declarations in a trembling voice tightly clasping my little hands, attempting to snatch a premature kiss from lips which I hoped would soon say a languid "yes" to me. I too —of a morning when the sun was young or in pale twilights of dawn—have stood waiting under windows for the beckoning of a white hand, the movement of a curtain, the flash of a light, the waving of a handkerchief. I too have written letters, hundreds of them, letters of poetry, and letters of despair, letters imploring and letters exalting—all sealed with the usual and the empty word (used by all lovers): *forever*. I have pressed other breasts to my breast. Many pairs of lips have I touched with my lips. Many pairs of eyes have I closed with my caresses. Every out-of-the-way street in my city brings a name to my mind, a flower, a word,—a name that I never mention now; a flower that lies crushed and dry between the pages of a discarded book; a word,—a word, alas, that I would so willingly forget!

Yes, dear lady, I too have been in love, and some women have—I take it for granted—loved me. I have given them pain and pleasure as other men have. I too know the fevers of anticipation, the agonies of uncertainty, the torments of doubt, the pains of expectancy, the tortures of jealousy, and the divine irresponsibility of a violent embrace when two souls try to tear each other from their bodies in an effort to become one soul.

If I refuse to speak of love it is not because I have not known it in all its degrees and in all its styles. I too have a soul, dear lady, a heart full of throbbing blood. I was not always insensitive to beauty. I was not born impotent, nor did I ever choose to become a eunuch.

As a child I knew all the terrors of chaste passion. As I grew older I, like all other men, regularly lost my chastity; I had my loves—illicit passions which my elders forbade, conventional engagements which my elders approved, and I landed—I, even I—at last in the lap of holy wedlock.

In view of all this you would be justified in asking me: "What more do you want?"

If you only knew, dear lady, what more I have wanted!

I have wanted, and I have never found, the ideal woman, the woman who really takes possession of a man and makes him over.

I have wanted, and I have never found, the woman who can take her place in the spiritual history of a soul, in the mental romance of a mind. "The eternal feminine leads us ever upwards." Perhaps it does, I am in no mood to quarrel with Wolfgang Goethe to-day. But I must say that so far as I am concerned, the eternal feminine has led me neither up nor down, neither this way nor that way, ever!

No, woman never appeared to me—either as a Beatrice who takes you by the hand and wakes you from your worldly dreams to lead you to realms celestial; or as a Circe, who changes men, born to virtue and to wisdom, into pigs rooting about in opulent gardens, rich in shade and in acorns.

Women neither corrupted me nor purified me. They were a side issue, so to speak, in my existence; guests, welcome or unwelcome, in my moments of leisure; hopes and promises of comfort in my hours of distress; purveyors, desired, of joy or pain; beloved, affectionate companions of unhappy days; intermezzi, voluptuous or passionate, in my hard studious life as a discontented laborer; extravagant, uncritical admirers of my work—but never, if I must be boorishly frank, never guides, benefactresses, inspirations, givers.

They took from me, they asked of me, and I gave them of my life, my youth, my time, my illusions, my thoughts; but they gave me nothing back. The story of my inner life was never enriched or changed by their presence in it.

I am not complaining! On the contrary: I gave because I had something to give—there was plenty, the larger part, left over for myself. I asked nothing of them for my mind or for my soul—they had nothing to give. I very well know that a woman, essentially and of necessity, is a parasite, a vampire, a thief. I took her for what she is. I took her as she is made. I let myself be robbed, and I promptly paid my tribute without haggling or bargaining.

In the final reckoning of joy and suffering we are quits. For pleasure received I rendered pleasure, for suffering inflicted I suffered in turn. For the rest I ask nothing; what is given is given. But so far as I know or see or remember they gave me nothing—just that: nothing; neither an idea, nor a bit of strength, nor yet an impetus toward those divine heights which my restless spirit has always sought to attain.

Such things should not be expected of a woman? That may be! I am inclined to think so myself. But in that case I am justified in not dealing with her in these pages, since I am writing only of a man's soul, and not of a whole man.

Or was it my fault that I did not succeed in finding or recognizing the Beatrice who might have exalted me to heaven? That is possible, very possible; and if it were true I would regret it more than all my sins, because a wondrous marvel indeed must be this exalter of men already predestined to exaltation!

But whether I did not meet her or, meeting her,

failed to understand her, she never descended from the heights to deify me; and so—well, I cannot say a word about her.

There, my dear, my impatient lady, there you have in a very few words the reasons for my silence on a subject which so deeply interests you. I realize only too well that the considerations which prompt my silence may be more offensive than silence itself; but how can I help that?

If I had been apt at lying or inventing, I might have passed this subject by, or else have contented you by inserting a spicy incident or two into this un-adorned narrative of the adventures of a soul. It is useless for me to try: I should not succeed. I cannot write what I do not feel, nor give a place to something that never had one.

And yet I would not have you dislike me altogether —you and other women who may perchance be willing to hear my story. I am going to give you a sample, just a wee, tiny sample, of the sort of thing my senti-mental recollections might have been. It concerns a memory of mine that is very far away—the first mem-ory of love indeed that I can count in my life.

An August night—long, long ago! We were walk-ing down the hill after one of the usual family dinners "beyond the gates." I had succeeded in falling behind —with *her,* the littlest, youngest, saddest, most neg-lected of all—the one most like me.

The white moon shining on the white dust of the roads, on the white houses, on the olive trees white behind freshly whitewashed walls, gave a strange almost theatrical dream-light to everything around us.

I tried to keep to the shadows; and as we were about to step out into the light again, my hand, long hesitant, reached out for hers, and then dropped it at once, with the sense of having done something dirty, something wrong.

My heart was beating too hard for a child of my age. The insistent and pathetic song of the crickets, scattered about, lost probably in the fields there, almost made me weep. I imagined their little black heads and feelers just emerging from holes in the ground under grass already cold with the evening dew; and it occurred to me that their rhythmic monotonous song was a cry for love and happiness, ever and again repeated in vain.

From that moment I too needed a little happiness; that very evening I at last had the courage to speak to her of things I had been thinking for so many months. Bit by bit the secret of my tormented nights came out in broken, halting phrases, under the unforgettable whiteness of that August moon. She listened to me quietly, her face white and motionless under the broad brim of her hat. She listened to me as though she were in a dream; but every now and then she would say "yes," "yes," and "yes" again without adding another word.

Deeply moved, I dressed up the details of my dreams as a diminutive philistine already mired in respectability: "As soon as we're grown up we'll get married, you and I. And we'll live in a little house all our own in the country, but not too far from town. We'll have an orchard and a garden not too small, with a great big bed of flowers, and in the middle of it, a pond for goldfish, and little yellow roses running over the iron gate. And the house will have a fine sitting-room, and in the sitting-room a clock with a shiny brass pendulum against the wall; and a round table with a red cloth; and the pictures of my father and mother and your father and mother in nice black frames lined with gold. And we'll have lots of pets: a fluffy white cat with a blue collar; pigeons in a house on the roof; three or four chickens for our eggs; a canary and a goldfinch in a cage—and we can hear them sing; and a big watchdog and, perhaps, a little monkey like the one the flower man keeps in the door of his shop on the corner. We'll spend all our time loving each other—"

And she: "Yes," "yes," nothing but "yes."

To her everything was natural, easy, simple. That we should spend all of our lives together, just we two, did not astonish her in the least.

Our future life I pictured as a laborious conquest, a distant ideal for attainment, a continuous struggle—serious business, in a word. To her it was different. She thought of it as noise, chatter, play time, a new game invented by me—the game of matrimony—the game of life. It's true she was a little pensive; but her pale face that had known but few caresses was unperturbed and serene. She did not understand me.

We did not understand each other. "Yes!" "Yes!"
She said "yes" precisely because she didn't understand.
And my own dream! How could it ever have been so
horribly petty, childish—so bourgeois! And I, I don't
know why, suddenly felt sadder than I would have had
she answered "no." So I dropped the subject and said
nothing more to her.

That was my first encounter with the soul of a
woman. The others were very different; and yet—

However; this is my last word on love in this story.
The very, very last! Take a bit of advice from me,
dear lady. Drop my book right here or throw it into
the waste-basket. And despise me, despise me—with
all your heart!

"Who has gone farthest?   For I would go farther."
                              WALT WHITMAN.

Chapter 22: My Mission

WHEN, after three or four years of capricious and reckless activity, I had achieved what most people would have deemed success (I had a name, I was read, discussed, followed, feared), I was more painfully conscious than before of a shameful emptiness within me.

What? Is that all?

Was that the ultimate objective of my days and nights of toil, the conclusion of my many-armed outreachings for a light less earthly? Was this the only, the final result of all my youth, of all my ardor and enthusiasm, repressed and concentrated over long years only to flare up into a sudden burst of flame, and then die out like a fire of straw kindled on a mountain top?

Was that all? Nothing but that? My name in print; my works quoted; my pictures in the magazines; my most cherished ideas made public property; my most intimate confessions, my most indiscreet enthusiasms, tossed on the market for the amusement of anybodies?

And then what? Monkeys around you repeating your every gesture; parrots around you repeating your every word; your name on the covers of books; your signature at the end of articles; your personality and character picked to pieces by people who do not understand you, who despise you, who envy you, but do not have the pluck to grind you under their heels! A famous author, even a quoted author; coddled by editors and publishers; pursued by reviewers and publicity agents; translated into foreign languages; a candidate for an honest, respectable, middle-aged celebrity?

And after that what? I was beginning to have all this and already to feel that it did not satisfy, that it would never satisfy me. What did I care about being, or becoming, a "brilliant" philosopher, a "writer well known in literary circles," a more or less successful manufacturer and retailer of words and ideas? Where was I going to end?

It wasn't hard to answer that. Looking ahead with all the mad anticipation which may be pardoned in nobodies, I could see myself on the road toward success with a first-class publisher—even Treves; a chair in some University; membership in some Academy, and perhaps some day (when I get old, decrepit, doddering enough) an award of the Nobel prize!

That? Not by a long shot! I felt that I had been born for something better than that, for higher aims than that. Mine was not ambition, it was not vanity: it was pride, but real honest pride, the pride of a Lucifer, the pride of a god! I wanted to be truly great, heroically great, epically great, immeasurably great. I wanted to accomplish something gigantic, unheard of, tremendous, something that would change the face of the earth and the hearts of men.

That or nothing! Otherwise—rot rather in the

brainless idleness of a government sinecure, or turn beast at manual labor, or—best of all—drown myself and my shattered dreams in the yellow water of the Arno!

My old persistent ambition to be chief, leader, guide, center! Old and persistent, but especially persistent during those days of achievements and eager strivings!

I confess: what I wanted—the reasons for wanting it mattered little—was that all eyes should be on me, at least for a moment; and that all lips should be speaking my name.

Founder of a school, leader of a faction, prophet of a religion, discoverer of theories or of extraordinary intellects, captain of a party, redeemer of souls, author of a best seller, master of a salon—anything, no matter what, so long as I was first, foremost, greatest, in Something!

To give my name to an idea or to a group of men; to disclose a new, unexpected, incredible truth; to be recognized, judged by people, to have my chapter in the histories or my paragraph in the encyclopedias; to have a field of my own, to stand for something that everybody must know!

No matter why, no matter how—but on no account should I be thrust aside, relegated to a second or a third row among interesting men, curious men, merely cultivated and intelligent. Something crazy, something foolish—never mind; so long as I was the lunatic of that lunacy, the fool of that folly!

At first I took under consideration that form of

action which superficial thinkers regard as the most active of all: politics. Socialism was already on the decline; but at that time it was still the most powerful movement operating in my country; and I, contrary by nature, born to minorities, came out against Socialism.

However, I became a Socialist, a Socialist upside down: I accepted the "class struggle." A real struggle, however, actual warfare, not just assault and battery practised by an emboldened and a hungry ruffian (the masses) upon an accommodating and chicken-hearted capitalism. The class struggle: the struggle of a class which has done things and which has won its power against a class trying prematurely to overthrow it: defense of the bourgeoisie—a defense knowing no pity; the policy of the mailed fist,—and all that goes with it: expansionism (Nationalism, that is, armament, an army and a navy). I became editor-in-chief of the leading Nationalist paper in Italy. I made a speech outlining the platform for a new Nationalist party. Every week I rioted with Popularists; started some new debate; assailed some Socialistic glory; disemboweled some revolutionary ideal—all to the end of restoring courage and dignity to a citizenry anxious only to surrender on easy terms. Italy was to regain her former greatness, even going in for wars of conquest. We thought of Africa. We asked for battleships. We tried to rekindle such sparks of Italy's expansionistic spirit as had survived the cold water of Adowa.

But I soon passed from this colonial and military imperialism to a spiritual nationalism. Italy seemed to me a country without life, without unity of ideals, without a common cause, stupefied, without red blood. Each for himself and graft for all! What was Italy's business in this world, what was her mission, I asked myself. I could find no answer. It was then that I began, with Mazzini's disregard of the proper moment, an inopportune "Campaign for an Awakening by Force." Faint trumpet blasts (articles, pamphlets, open letters) in a world thinking of something else! I wanted my country to do something on her own account, play a distinctive individual rôle among the nations. I wanted Italians to forget the rhetoric of a *Risorgimento* dead and buried, and start working out a great national destiny, a glorious common cause. Since 1860 there had been no united Italian thought, no real sentiment that was Italian. The time had come to be up and doing. A nation that is not moved by some Messianic passion is foredoomed to crumble.

What was this national goal to be? I was not so sure myself. I cried out, I appealed to the many who had rallied to my call. My message was this: We must make way for the dominion of Mind over Things. In Italy Mind has always been recognized; therefore the reign of Mind must begin with us!

But could Mind be a principle of national cohesion? I soon discovered that it couldn't. The problem of the absolute dominion of Will soon overstepped the most fantastic patriotism. All men had to be considered. All men had to be worked for. There could be no question of the material physical interests of an acre or two of the earth's surface, but rather of the spiritual interests of all humanity.

I was convinced to the bottom of my soul that I had a mission in the world—my own mission, a great mission. It seemed to me that I was called upon every day to do what others had left undone, to change men and things in the twinkling of an eye, to divert the peaceful course of history.

Who had called me? I did not know, I do not know.

I did not believe in God; and yet there were moments when I felt like a Christ obligated at all hazards to promote a new redemption. I did not believe in Providence; and yet I saw myself as a future Messiah and Savior of mankind. Voices spoke within me—deep cavernous voices that seemed to rise from a nether hemisphere, another earth. I imagined that already this life of ours was *another life* and this earth a heaven for people groaning below (not dead as yet down there, not born as yet up here); and I thought that they were calling on me to save them, lift them to my level, that they might share in our diviner joys, our more certain truths. At times I felt much as a god must feel when he hears a multitude praying at his feet for happiness and liberation, death and redemption. At such moments I was moved as I never had been at a reading of Matthew, Mark, Luke, and John. Once I broke into tears over a simple, matter-of-fact account of the life of Mazzini.

I was mysteriously impelled to do something for men—for *all* men. Somehow I felt as though I had given a promise and that the hour of fulfilment could no longer be postponed.

I had made myself; I must now make others. I had destroyed; I must now rebuild. I had despised reality; I must now renovate, purify it. I had hated men; I must now love them, sacrifice myself for them, make them like gods.

Otherwise, what was I born for? Why else had I sternly denied the past? Either start at the beginning, make everything over, sublimate everything through a supreme effort of love and will, make reality habitable even for the most delicate and for the greatest souls, or else renounce everything—from the instinctive enjoyments of a vegetative life to the satisfactions of being a semi-celebrity in Europe and America! Even in the field of action I was again confronted with the old dilemma of my boyhood: everything or nothing!

Knowledge alone no longer satisfied me now: I demanded action. Nor was writing quite enough: I had to impress my will upon things and upon people. I wanted to get away from ceaseless thinking; from juggling with dead words and cold concepts; from mental fireworks—systems set up and taken down day by day; from rockets of paradox; from pin-wheels of fancy. I was tired of observing, judging, commenting on what others were doing—tired of just criticizing and tearing down. The world of thoughts, words, and paper in which I was performing seemed arid, hopeless, sterile to me now. The time had come to leave it for something vaster, more concrete, more constructive.

Not, however, for the primitive animal life of everybody and anybody; not for "business"; not for the ordinary occupations of people; not for any action that was simply continuation and repetition; not for that struggle that is a struggle for bread, for house-rent, for money, for women, and for power over others. I wanted to act, but not on an ordinary human plane like anybody else. There was something far different to be done and no one was doing it. Live, yes, but not the usual placid monotonous life! Act, yes, but not with the old purposes in view! My passage across this planet must leave a deeper impression than any revolution, any earthquake. My desire was, in short, that *with me, through my work, a new age in the history of mankind should begin*. A new era, an epoch wholly different from all other periods, a Third Kingdom!

Man, in the beginning, had been pure beast, an animal living a wholly vegetative physical life. From that plane he had risen to humanness: he had made tools, brought fire, the wind, other animals, to serve him. Little by little he had freed his mind from exclusive concern with self-preservation: he had enlightened and exalted himself in art. But human life was still encumbered with survivals, legacies from his brute condition: take off the gentleman's tailor-made suit, deprive him of the mechanical appliances which he has developed to perfection, and you get a very passable barbarian. His common purposes and ideals have not much changed from those of his brigand ancestors: good eating; possession of the most beautiful women; bullying of the weak; stealing as much as possible from others not so weak. The supreme and truly super-animal joys of thought for thought's sake, of pure disinterested thought, the enjoyment, comprehension, and creation of art, belong to a few, and to those few often for a few moments only. Humanity, therefore, is in a stage halfway between brute and hero, between Caliban and Ariel, between the bestial and the divine. My task accordingly was to wrest it from that ambiguous position, free it from that contamination. All that man retained of the infra-man must be killed, suppressed, extirpated, that he might stand forth in his glory as more than man, as superman, exalted to godship, incarnating true divinity, multitudinously alive in the Spirit and through the Spirit.

What is the highest, purest, noblest part of man? The mind! Well, then, to act on man in a direction of improvement, you must act on his mind. Only along spiritual lines is a complete and radical evolution, a total transformation of all beings and all values, to be hoped for. Man can reach the heights only through his better self. His present spiritual life already contains the seed, the beginnings, of the divine life that awaits him. The contemplation of the philosopher, the ecstasy of the mystic, the creation of the poet—all those things which carry us away from the humiliating necessity of self-preservation, from the hideous whirl of earthly interests—are functions of the Spirit. And the Spirit is flexible, malleable, perfectible. It holds infinite promises and unhoped-for surprises in reserve, and gives evidence of containing the germs of other faculties still, the requisites for progress toward miraculous developments. If anything new and great is to come of man it will come of the Spirit; if we are going to perfect man, we must first perfect the Spirit. The Spirit encompasses all values, all the justifications of bodily life, all the motives of our acts. If the Spirit were suddenly to change, all life would change. If it were to seek different ends, if it abandoned some of its predilections and took up with others, human existence would be revolutionized and regenerated. All questions, national, social, moral, are at bottom nothing but questions of Mind, spiritual questions. Transform the internal, and the external is transformed; renovate the Mind and the world is renovated.

That the world needed such renovation I did not doubt. The life men were leading—slow, heavy, somnolent, vulgar, physical, hellish—nauseated me more and more. I wished others to feel this nausea and find the strength to rise above it, reducing the importance of the life of the body, repudiating the traditional manner of living—a savage barbarous thing, ill disguised (in fact rendered actually more hideous) by steel and electricity.

That man should mount at least one step higher was indispensable. A new volume of universal history must at last be opened. In the beginning man was flesh; then he was flesh and spirit; now he must be all spirit, spirit alone. Following on the Age of Beasts and the Age of Men—the Age of Heroes, Gods, Angels! First the era of force, then the era of intelligence in the service of force; finally liberated Intelligence, Will Predominant, Mind the Master of all forces.

To lead men toward this Kingdom, to herald the dawn of this new age, to bring this new epoch into being, such was the duty which I voluntarily took upon myself. Mine was a double mission: to disgust men with their present mode of life and wean them from it; to prepare and exemplify the superhuman life which I presensed and ever dimly visualized with all the exasperated tenseness of supreme desires.

And how should I set about this? Was I worthy of assuming such a task? Would I succeed in it? Was I myself so permeated with the Spirit, so dominated by the Spirit, that I had the right to preach to others and to impose on others a life less entangled with ugliness and evil?

And though my mind were clean, virtuous, without stain or weakness, would I have an intellect sturdy enough and resourceful enough to inspire in others the will to break—as it would be necessary to break—with their thoughtless hand-to-mouth existence, to encompass the elevation of hundreds of nations to the sphere of the Divine?

To begin on my mission I had first to be sure of myself. I had to purify myself and make myself a greater man, attain moral perfection and intellectual sublimity, make myself a saint and a genius!

Chapter 23 : Perfect!

WHAT? Is there not one among you who has the courage to come to my house, meet me face to face, and tell me frankly, pitilessly, without sugaring the pill, just what I am? Is there not one among you who will tell me baldly, in true friendship, what I have done that is wrong, what I have left undone that I should have done, my defects, my vices, my crimes? Are you all cowards and hypocrites—fussy, harmless old ladies of fifty? You're afraid I don't mean it? You think I'll take offense at what you say, that instead of throwing my arms about you and thanking you I'll break your heads and put you out of doors?

Out with it, gentlemen, in God's name! Have you never seen the face of an honest man who dares speak the truth? From the bottom of my heart, from the depths of my soul's misery I appeal to you, I entreat you! I must know! I need to know what wrong I have done that I may repent of it and pay the penalty. I must know, at all costs, what my faults are that I may uproot them, burn them, be rid of them. Don't you see? Don't you understand what it is that is tormenting me, eating my heart out, day and night?

I want to become a great soul, a great man, pure, noble, *perfect*. I know that I have this one life to live and I intend to live it well. The lives you people lead disgust me. I intend either to be great or to kill my-self! There is no other choice for a man such as I. I need to be above you that I may raise you higher than you are. But to become great I must harrow, and torment, and polish, and magnify the soul that has been given me (I know not by whom) for the few years I am to spend as a visitor, as an exile, on this earth. But before you can make a soul great, you must know wherein it is small; to make it clean you must see wherein it is dirty; to make it courageous and strong you must drag all its fears and shrinkings out into the light of day.

Do you think I have not been looking at myself enough? Do you imagine I have not spied warily, cunningly, relentlessly, on all the motives, second thoughts, afterthoughts, evasions, self-deceptions, impulses, tremors, of my heart?

And yet—lift your eyebrows if you will, call me a liar if you will—I have found NOTHING! Understand? Nothing! I have found nothing that disgusts me or that fills me with shame. In all these years I have not been able to find one single defect that was surely a defect, one single vice that was unquestionably a vice. Never have I been able to stop on the verge of an act of mine and say: "This is a vile thing to do!" Not even once have I felt a twinge of remorse at something I had failed in doing or at something contrary to the laws of men or of God that I had done.

But tell me the truth for once at least. Tell me—I beg you in the name of all you hold most dear—was there ever a man in my condition? Is it possible? Am I a saint without sin? Am I the one virtuous man, the one spotless soul, the one perfect human being?

Is it possible? Don't believe it for a minute! It is *im*possible, the most impossible of all impossibilities! Certainly! I too must be bad, dirty, cowardly, weak, untruthful, heartless, a bluff, a sham! I too must be sinning seventy times seven times a day, with a soul as black and stinking as a cesspool. Otherwise—well, I would not be a man. Otherwise—why should I feel forever surging up in every part of me this enormous desire I have to be a great soul, a beautiful soul?

No, my friends, it is useless to wheedle me with little words of flattery whispered in my ear. I do not believe you, I will never believe you. I may be pure in your eyes. You could call anything pure for all the morals you have, morals of beggars and traitors, morals of idlers trying to excuse your laziness—of hogs dressed up as men! But not in my eyes! Not in my eyes am I pure and great! Nor in thine eyes, O incomparable Ideal of my life, am I as I would be, as I must be, to approach death with firm step and head high!

The fact is . . . the fact is that no one can know himself—no one can see severely enough, nor tell frankly enough, what he really feels, and thinks, and does. Pride is a shrewd deceiver. Vanity is a sly minx. Self-interest is a cool calculator. Shame will never face the music. Self-respect is a ready liar! And they are always on hand to hide, to soften, to attenuate, to excuse, to justify. That must be why I cannot recognize the rot that is in me. That must be why I see myself as the white swan of perfection!

So now you understand! Now you see why I need you and cannot do without your uttermost severity. It takes others to see what is bad in a man: the spite native to human beings has sharp eyes and a ready mind. Nothing escapes its accursed vigilance. What it does not see it guesses, and what it cannot guess it invents. Men have always been quick at finding the mote in their neighbor's eyes.

You can't imagine what I'm talking about? Excuse me! This is not the time for side-stepping nor for compliments. You see right into me! And probably you are disgusted with what you see—you experts in holy horror! But is there not *one* among you who will talk to me, not one, not even one, who will come and tell me everything? I assure you: I am not like other people. I vomit at praise. I despise adulation. I cannot endure euphemisms and evasions.

Perhaps you are afraid? The first man who calls my attention to a fault I shall think of as my savior, my dearest friend, my real brother.

Perhaps my case is too hopeless! Perhaps you think you would not have time or patience to tell the whole story? Please, make the sacrifice! I will pay you for your trouble as best I can. I will give you all I possess: I will steal and give you the proceeds. I will crawl on my belly into your houses to serve and worship you.

You can't see anything wrong? Then you are blind

and stupid, because if the evil is there, you—out-siders—should detect it at a glance. Put on your glasses! Stir up that spite of yours (you have plenty of it)! Follow me around! Catch me off my guard! Anything you like—provided only you denounce me, accuse me, without mercy! My life or my death, my greatness or my abjectness, lie in your hands.

What are you muttering there among yourselves? Ah, of course! That is your way! You talk only be-hind people's backs! You flay them in secret! You slander them under your breath! You point them out when they are not looking! But that won't do—in my case! Come out in the open! Step out into the light! Speak so you can be heard! I am not ashamed! I will not run away! I want to be accused, defamed, that I may rise to a certain place I have my eye on!

Oh, I see. . . . Perhaps—no offense, I assure you! —perhaps you refuse to show me my defects because you prefer to keep me from being better than you, from attaining that perfection which I am looking for! In that case . . .

I appeal to you, men, all men, friends and enemies alike; have mercy on me, a poor lost soul athirst for greatness! Do not withhold from me the bitter cup of condemnation! Speak without reserve; arraign me ruthlessly! Do not stop if my eyes fill with tears! Do not lose courage if my face grows pale! I shall kill myself if you do not point out my sins and shortcomings to me, if you do not tell me at once how despicable and vile I am! On my knees I beseech you, all men of the earth: have the courage for once to tell the truth, the whole truth, the naked truth!

Chapter 24: A Man of Genius!

PEOPLE all around keep telling me that I am a genius, and they, good souls, think they are doing me a great honor and giving me a great pleasure in so saying. A few even say that I am a great genius, and these are the men who think they are my best friends and stand closest to me.

I tip my hat to you, kind people, and may God reward you for your kindness! You are saying and doing all you can say and do; you are even able, for a moment, to swallow your own vanity and overlook my ill-mannered ways.

Is there not one among you who knows how much and how bitterly you hurt me with this talk of genius (*ingegno*)?

To the devil with all your genius! What are you talking about? Do you really think I can rest content with being a "man of genius," a "boy of promise" (promising and promising till the undertaker gets him!), an amusing chap, witty, and interesting? What, if you please, do you take me for? Have I the insipid, good-natured face of the man who is satisfied if he has what others have, who is happy if there are ten ideas on his tongue and a hundred francs in his pocketbook? Have you never noticed, you ravens of ill omen, that brains are the cheapest and commonest commodity on sale in the public market? And especially here in

Italy, as everybody knows! Tell me, if you can; who, in this land blessed of the gods, is without "genius"? Find me such a man, and I'll give you his weight in gold! Brains, donkeys mine, run in every Italian street, flood every Italian house, overflow from every Italian book, spout from every Italian mouth. Brains make up the muck that oozes in every Italian cellar.

"A lad of genius! Too bad he doesn't do anything!"

"See that fellow there? A scoundrel, a cheat, but, I will tell you, a man of genius!"

"Yes, I agree with you! He does talk a lot of nonsense! But you can't deny it: he is a 'man of genius.'"

Such are the remarks one hears every day in Italy; on the sidewalks, in people's houses, in the restaurants, wherever the so-called intellectuals congregate.

Genius! Any one who can write a verse, or rhyme a song, with an agreeable cadence here and there and a passable rhythm, is a "man of genius." If you paint a few flowers in water color (and make them look real!) you are a "man of genius"! If you can do a piece on the piano, in front of a bust of Beethoven, you are a "man of genius." If you can describe the ravages of an earthquake with a certain elegant sentimentality you are a "man of genius." Designers of ice-cream cones are "men of genius," as well as dilettanti "of the future," who talk about what others do, shooting streams of ideas and streams of smoke in parallel lines toward the ceiling.

I ask you again: who among us is without "genius"? Even those who do nothing at all are "men of genius," even our politicians, even our journalists . . .

Let me say it therefore once and for all: to tell me I am a genius is to insult me. To tell me that I am a genius is to give me not a pleasure but a pain.

I have no use for your genius. I put it with my waste paper and send it to the back-house. Frankly speaking I consider *your* "genius" merely as the upper grade of mediocrity. Your genius is that higher form of intelligence which every one can understand, appreciate and love. Genius is that salted and peppered mixture of facility, wit, and information, of decorated commonplace, of exhilarated philistinism, which is so palatable to ladies, schoolmasters, lawyers, celebrities, and men of the world, in fact, to all the betwixts and betweens—people neither in heaven nor in hell, equidistant from downright imbecility and from real genius.

Let them be, these men of genius! May they be successful, enjoy themselves, have a good time in life, and amuse people! I am not one of them, nor do I care to be.

Nothing but extremes ever satisfy me. Where living beings are concerned I like only perfect animals, or perfect vegetables, such as do their work honestly, knowing nothing else, without flitting about here and there in a stew of chatter and ambition—or else real geniuses, great minds, heroes, solitary, gigantic as a mountain at night!

A peasant or a Dante!—away with all who are in

between; get out from under my feet, you men of genius, you men of talent, you men of ability, you clever, witty, skilful, loathsome intellectuals! What are you in comparison with the grimy toiler who grinds the grain that gives you bread; or in comparison with the poet who squeezes from his soul words that make a thousand generations think and shudder? What do you produce? Words and words! Playthings, toys— bluff!

My choice is already made. Even though I wished to, I could not be a tree or a laborer; but I do want, I do will desperately, to be a really great man. Let me say it in a word that should strike terror to the heart: I want to be *a genius!* Not *ingegno,* mere talent, but *genio,* a real genius!

If I fall by the roadside without achieving my desire, I will accept my sad destiny and weep where none can see. I will crawl into some little corner of the world to die alone, like the brave wolf of De Vigny! But I will *not* be prostituting myself among those I have despised.

I will repent of nothing. I am sure I will experience such joys even though I do not succeed—the joys of feeling my soul clean and set toward something as sublime as it is absurd—that I shall not even notice the stones I trip over on the road, nor hear the laughter of the man who is "cultivating his garden" and thinks it a world.

Be not downcast, O my soul courageous, if many a time you seem stupid and ignorant. Genius is not what they call "brilliant." It does not pass pretty ideas around like plates of tea and toast. It does not keep up with the latest magazines and the best selling books. Quite the contrary!

The genius is a child, and mad. The genius is a genius because he has the courage to be a lunatic and a child. He cannot help seeming ignorant and idiotic at times; for he wonders at many simple things and talks often without common sense.

But only to the genius, O soul of mine, do those marvelous hours come when God himself seems to be speaking through your mouth, when all is light, when everything stands revealed, limpid, and harmonious as the water of a beautiful stream—hours when the soul is like fire, like air, like love—hours when, through some mysterious madness, everything is possible and everything is sacred, and you cannot tell which is soul —your soul—and which is world.

Ho, you people! Don't you see what a dull and insipid trifle your genius is as compared with such moments of real genius? To have one such hour I would give all the genius you credit to me and all the genius of all the buffoons in the world!

And even then I should probably feel that I had stolen it!

Chapter 25: Dies Irae

DESPERATE cries these, shouted in the void, addressed to others, but uttered to myself! Struggles, self-mortifications, writhings of remorse! Sublime resolves fizzling out in three thousand words for a newspaper! Fevers of purity at once forgotten in the white arms of a woman! Assaults on heights sublime; stormings of embattled heavens; thirst for dangerous adventure and the "grand emprise"; leaps of a man out toward another life, a life beyond life; dethronings of gods; fulfilments of the serpent's promise; real redemption, without a cross and without red blood dripping from white hands of benediction! Unceasing, maddening, uncontrollable dreams of miracles! And meantime— a small, petty, pious, daily life, in a small room, in a cheap café, in a small city, among very small people!

And yet I struggled. I fought bravely, valiantly, my heart filled with all hope, my mind with all good-will. I had pledged my whole being: Be this! Do that! Else—disappear! I struggled against the temptations enticing me towards a bread-winning mediocrity. I strove to create around me a ruthless solitude of spirit if not of body. I fought myself. I punished myself. I inured myself to pain for the terrible trials that were to come. I felt the need of concentrating utterly in my inner, my innermost Self, of withdrawing into a silence where I could hear my own voice and nothing else. I was to be the first man of the new humanity—I was to set the first example of a wholly spiritual life, a life independent of body, of matter, of animalness.

The goal I had set for myself was, I soon discovered, still remote; and I was not as yet that spirit without blemish or weakness, which was predestined to show men the road to the life beyond. But I was not discouraged on that account. The enthusiasm born of the very absurdity of my undertaking; the bold aspiration that made the grandest dreams of men seem small; the mad certainty I felt of future success; the titanic pride which filled me at the thought that I was the instrument chosen to carry out a mission so unusual and so marvelous as I pictured it; the absolute necessity of my breaking away from this reality, this world, this humanity—all added day by day to my blindness, as I rushed headlong toward the most horrible awakening that could await a mortal man. I seemed to be striding across the earth like an invisible giant, stepping from mountain peak to mountain peak, leaping the green seas—so vast and lonely—like so many puddles, my head among the stars of heaven, warming myself at the fire of the sun as the wanderer does at a camp-fire of burning twigs.

The most incredible, the most lurid visions crowded through my mind during those days, the wilder rushing in to replace the less wild in a crescendo of mad paroxysms even more intense.

But the fixed underlying thought was always one and the same: to make possible, desirable, imminent the palingenesis of man, the transfiguration of the beast-man, the universal advent of the god-man. But first of all, others must begin to feel what I was feeling. They too must be filled with contempt, horror, terror, shame, for the ambiguous amphibious lives they and I were leading.

And then I thought of art.

Art alone could perform the miracle. Poetry alone could sharpen that disgust for the pettiness in our lives, which is so frequently dulled by habit. Poetry alone could rearouse terror, rekindle remorse, reawaken the sense of shame, and create the pain of the unbearable in souls comfortably settled in pleasant compromise. Thinking, theory, could not do it. Thinking convinces only a few; it is an actual bore to the majority; but art, living art, poetry, the poetry that grips you, subdues you (poetic poetry, that is, with all its color and harmony and irresistible directness)—they could do it—they could force men to see themselves mirrored in the dead sea of human existence, and to shrink from their ugliness in horror, in a sudden desire to escape from it, to be *different*. For Narcissus the sight of his own image reflected in a flower-framed pool meant death; for humanity the same experience would be the beginning of a new life.

At that time poetry could not be for me (in my prevailing state of mind) anything miniature, episodic, limited. I was living in an atmosphere of greatness, thinking great things. Even poetry, though a first rough instrument of redemption and nothing more, had to be great, very great, as great as possible. Great at least in conception—great as canvas, as picture: a cosmic poem, a universal drama, a vast scene. Looking back over my readings I could think of but two books worthy of attention in the sense I meant: the "Divine Comedy" and "Faust"—both of them gigantic bird's-eye views of life and history, of the Now and of the Hereafter. In Dante, the world below and the world above, for judgment on the world we live in; in Goethe, the world of myth and speculation, for judgment on the world of reality. Sorrow and Love; the Above and the Below; Saints and Mothers; and a whirlwind sweeping along between heaven and earth, with a mortal sinner groping for Salvation.

But neither the book of the Prior of Florence nor the book of the Counselor of Frankfurt was what I wanted. The two legends—the legend of eternal life and the legend of eternal youth—were not subjects vast enough to embrace the whole life of all men in all its aspects and phases. Something more was needed, something greater, much greater! In Christianity I found another myth better suited to my purposes: *The Day of Judgment.* So I outlined, in my mind and on paper as well, the one tragedy in tune with my madness: the *Dies Irae,* the day of wrath, the day of fear, the day of the gnashing of teeth, the day of last judgment—judgment on the first man and on the last man!

The sun had grown as white as the moon in a sky that seemed vaster and blacker than ever; and the earth was shriveled and shrunken like a piece of fruit left forgotten on its tree. And men had taken refuge in caves and catacombs under the earth, where they lived closer to their dead, huddled together like sheep at the approach of winter. Spring came again and brought no flowers. The last nightingale died in its lonely nest. The oxen, weary of their æon-long toil, were naught but white bones stretched out in repose on unplowed fields. The deserted cities of stone, of marble, of steel, were crumbling bit by bit in the darkness, the silence, and the solitude.

One man only refused to give up hope of Heaven. His brothers all had long since renounced the superstition which came out of Palestine and took its name from the Christ. He alone believed. He alone, the last of the Christians, stood on a hilltop waiting for those signs which, as all Scripture had promised, would portend the Great Ending. And, behold, his faith conquered! The Revelation of John came true before tired eyes that had sleeplessly watched so long. Black horses galloped across the devastated earth. The seas hurled their waters toward the sky and waves beat on the mountain tops. The heavens opened at last and myriads of flaming darts came raining through the wounds in the black vault, burying the lands that had escaped the flood in a deluge of fire. Then, when the signs seemed certain, the last of the Christians went down into the caverns beneath the earth and called to his brothers: "The end has come! The dread day has broken! David and the Sybil prophesied not in vain! We must prepare ourselves! The Day of Judgment is at hand! The day of wrath is upon us!"

But the men did not wish to die. They could not believe in death, in an end, in a Judgment. The Christian's voice rang out. They tried not to hear him, but his words troubled every heart. Then some remembered that this man's God had died on a cross. So in mockery of his belief he too was crucified—that his voice might be stilled. As the nails pierced his hands and his blood ran down in thick drops and his nude torso writhed in agony, he once again foretold the approaching End, the imminent, inevitable End. When Death had sealed his lips all men felt free and happy. They threw themselves into an orgy of joy down there in the caverns under the earth; and the last day of the world was like a hell of wicked indulgences. But soon great abysses yawned under their feet; mountains were torn asunder with the noise of a thousand thunders; the vaults of the caves fell in; and all the earth was a pit of the dead, a vast charnel in which there was no living soul.

Silence reigned.

There were hours (or centuries?) of silence—as it was in the beginning. The great spherical sepulcher whirled along its orbit in Nothingness, with all the peacefulness of its graves. All voices were silent; all problems were solved; all burdens were lifted; and the dead could rest in peace at last; for there was no one orchestra; my chorus, the assembled races of the earth, and my language, something new, formidable, mighty, perfect, clear, made up of all the sounds known to the world, from the crooning of a baby to the thunder of a waterfall. The groans and sobs would shake the firmament; the shouts would be the shouts of nations calling from their knees; and my silences, real silence, the Silence that is never attained by man! And all men would tremble at reading, or seeing, or listening to my poem. And in that final scene, so powerfully imagined, they would recognize their whole life, with all its good and all its evil: a life that runs on without a resurrection to the day of wrath when all would be brought to judgment—but a judgment by men under a heaven empty of gods! And in the terror occasioned then by my monstrous drama men would feel the need of a new kind of life—the life promised by me!

living to disturb them, no one living to remember them, or to miss them, or to weep for them.

But then, of a sudden—a blast of trumpets—the terrible trumpets of the Resurrection! Trumpets, sharp and shrill, magic trumpets, trumpets never conceived by man! Trumpets of a blast so mighty, so piercing, so thunderous, so commanding, that the dead awakened—even the dead who had slept for a thousand, for ten thousand years. Heavenly trumpets, sounded by lips unknown, as potent as the gentlest word of Christ; so moving, so quickening, that at their sound the dead deep buried under earth and sea were stirred, so untiring, so insistent, that flesh was formed again about the skeletons of the dead, and life, breath, and motion, returned to them. A limitless army of Resurrected Dead!

Lo the Valley of Jehoshaphat, large as the world, stretching from ocean to ocean, and covered, filled, overflowing, with all that risen humanity, those men, those women, those children, of all ages, of all countries, of all colors, of all eras, brothers born on the same planet, meeting for the first time. And they cried out in fear and trembling: they were *waiting!*

Most of them did not know why they were there; so they asked and could not understand each other. Some stood apart by themselves, weeping. Some hid their faces that they might not see. Some found themselves again, recognized who they were, and remembered—and their fellows too. They conversed at last, the first *true* conversations among men.

The things we dream of now came true. Cæsar could speak with Alexander; Dante embraced Virgil; Charles the Fifth put questions to Solomon. Soldiers met soldiers; kings met kings; fair women were with their lost lovers again. Peasants who were born and died alone on the mountains gathered in groups and made signs—the sign of the cross—to each other.

At last they all knew why they had been awakened and what was in store for them. The true Christians exulted. The hour had come when they should see Christ, their Christ, descend from the clouds to punish and reward. Here and there people had already begun to pray, to excuse themselves, to beg for mercy, to plead in desperation for final forgiveness. There were some who still found courage to menace the absent gods. A few held that this posthumous awakening was one last taunt of Destiny before real annihilation. Others suggested that houses be built and a government formed. Men and women could be seen on the ground, their arms wrapped about each other in embraces that would let them forget their terror.

They did not understand each other. No one understood what he himself was saying. Every second some voice would be raised in an effort to make itself heard; and a thousand other voices would answer. Soon the tumult was so unbearable that they all were obliged to join in. Prophets were still trying to ply their trade. One went up to a hilltop and began to exhort excitedly without once stopping for breath, though no one paid the slightest attention to what he was saying.

Finally they were all worn out. The judgment did not begin. They waited there in silence, long hours, long days, maybe years. And still no one came. Then they all cried in unison:

"Christ!" "Christ!" "CHRIST!"

The united voices of all humanity, of every human being who had lived on earth, loving, suffering, hoping, rose as a challenge toward heaven. Judgment! Judgment! They demanded judgment! The horrors of uncertainty were more terrible than the horrors of Hell itself.

A poor man told of the life of the poor and asked to be allowed to die again; a king told of the lives of kings; a poet of the lives of poets; a laborer of the lives of laborers; a prostitute of the lives of prostitutes; a sailor of the lives of sailors. Chinese peasants, Egyptian slaves, Indian warriors from America, legionaries of Rome, miners of England, each told of the hard lives they had lived. And they all asked for mercy: they all asked to die again.

Who among them had been happy? Who among them had been sinful? Life had never given them what they asked! And the greater part of them had lived ever in the dark: God had spoken only to the elect! Who had made them as they were? And what was this joke of a Resurrection? Was it to lead to a better and more beautiful life? If not, death were better, ah, yes, far better!

After this great cry from billions of unfortunate souls, a great silence fell. Even the Christians wavered at last. Why did not Christ appear in His glory, in the midst of the heavens, seated on a throne of fire, surrounded by angels and saints, as in the pictures painted by the monks of old?

But at last a voice was heard calling above the silent multitude; and the voice said: "Christ is not in heaven. Christ is among you, humble and alone. He too was a man. He too is awaiting judgment. Let men be the judges of men and to each be given the destiny which he believed in. Those who believed in Paradise will be blessed in Paradise; and those who believed in death shall return to ashes and dust."

And men once more fell asleep—this time forever.

There was a great deal more that I cannot remember to-day! But how ridiculous it all seems now—this imperfect outline of a tragedy that would have been the first wholly tragic tragedy ever written! "Faust"? "Faust" was nothing compared to mine! Imagine! A thousand dialogues! A hundred thousand scenes—all of life, with all its characters, through all the ages. The history of the universe in dramatic form! The Comedy Divine and the Tragedy Infernal brought to completion and enlarged to the impossible!

I dreamed of seeing my drama performed on a stage as big as the Sahara, with real mountains for scenery. The words were to have the tremendous force of Dante's. The actors would be heroic figures like the statues of Michelangelo. The music would have a grander sweep than the music of Wagner. The wind would be the breath behind my voice; the sea, my

Chapter 26: Action?

PHILOSOPHY! Desire and hope for the certain knowledge that brings peace; sacred gateway to inaccessible truths; philter of ascetic enthusiasms in the empty Thebaids of systems; Dionysiac substitute for the normal empirical experience of things, for physical joys, for amusements (consolations?) to be bought for cash!

Philosophy! Friend of my childhood; love of my boyhood; passion of my youth! Faith without Scriptures; worship without ceremonies; communion without prayer—yet nearer and dearer to my heart than all religions! Abstract thought, as plain and unadorned as the masterpieces of the Primitives; pure idea, more harmonious, more perfect than any creature; pure concept, as unilinear as the line that makes a first design on the unsoiled canvas of Being!

Philosophy! Magic worlds peopled with phantoms more alive than living men; with shadows more satisfying than substances; with words more solid than things, and formulas more stirring than strophes of poetry!

I knew thee, I loved thee, I raped thee! Thou wert a bounteous table spread before me in my season of fasting. Thou wert a consuming fever in my excess of health. Thou didst sing an unforgettable song in the desert of my heart!

196

Brain, brain, all brain! Theories, principles, dialectics—abstractions, nothing but abstractions! Systems were the food I lived on. Systems were the life I lived. Metaphysics was the bread I ate. Metaphysics was the dreams I dreamed!

My Eden was a tanglewood of thorny ideologies, in which not a leaf was green! The dazzling sun of celestial unity beat upon my head, already hot with congested blood and congested reasoning, with a light that hurt my blinded eyes and closed them with the violence of its splendor. In that wilderness of dead wood and brambles I, like the anchorites of old, came to know the fleshly torments of sensual worldly beauties. Women looked steadily at me with their large, black, wide-open eyes. On sunny seashores the golden oranges of Goethe swayed, dangling to and fro in breezes heavy with salt and Infinitude. And for long years (many, many years, many, many months, many, many days—and nights!) I was faithful unto thee, as faithful as a paladin to his emperor. I had no other God before thee. I sought thee out in all books; I revered thee in all forms; I saw thee in all words; I conquered thee as my possession in the great; I became thy defender in the small. At each discovery my spirit rejoiced in triumph; for each advance upon the stronghold of truth I wrestled, I struggled, body to body, hand to hand. For every sudden burst of light, long nights of delirious thinking!

To thee, Philosophy, I owe my all: my longing for purified worlds; my ecstatic flights into the realms of understanding; my adeptness in annihilations; my feeling of superiority over the man in the street. I belonged wholly to thee, and for me thou wert everything!

And yet a moment came when I saw thee as thou wert: a labored aureole of mystic hen's tracks scrawled around a zero; a vain and changing order imposed upon an unorderable ever-evasive flux; an ironical madcap race toward thine own destruction!

And I renounced thee, I reviled thee, I cast thee off —I was false unto thee! Thou wert a stone in my pathway of attainment! Thy promises thou didst not keep with me, or—when thou didst honor them they availed me not! I willed to act, to do, to change—to transform the reality of to-day into the reality of to-morrow. But thou gavest me only futile contemplation, the immobility of the absolute, the wearying excitement of impatient dashes upon a goal ever receding before me!

Philosophy had been knowledge (contemplation) and a seeking for the universal (unity).

Instead, I wanted action (change, creation), and therefore reality (immediate concrete reality: the particular). I reversed the age-old conception of philosophy from All to Nothing. I broke with tradition and went back to "prephilosophy." In so doing I thought I was benefiting the philosophy of the philosophers. Every problem I came to regard as a problem of instruments—of the transformation of instruments. Philosophers had tried only to find new solutions to old problems; but all solutions, past and present, had been developed from the same premises, following the same laws, succumbing to the same fallacies— the products, in fact, of very similar mental processes.

It was useless to go any farther along those well-worn paths. An experience repeated over centuries and centuries gave ample warning—in the poverty and insignificance of its results—that nothing more could be done or hoped for in those directions. Improved terminologies, revamped methods, partial repairs to the machinery of logic—these were pitiable makeshifts of people unable to strike out courageously for themselves from the King's Highways of their fathers. If new conquests were to be made, in order to hope justifiably for arriving at any certain truth, to obtain results truly and radically different from the usual ones, it would be necessary to choose the hard but only possible alternative of making a fresh start from a different angle. Philosophy is a structure built with tools. The tools which philosophy must use are the brains of philosophers. A better output can be had only from better tools. Therefore, to improve philosophy the brains of philosophers must be improved. It is a question of reforming *souls*.

That is to say: we must do something, we must act, we must alter—and not rest content with just knowing, thinking, describing.

Philosophers (and not all of them either—only a very, very few) have so far thought of changing only one of their tools: language. They have not thought of the most important tool of all: the soul.

The same principle could be applied to ethics. Why multiply the norms, rules, commandments, imperatives, already existing, if men snapped their fingers at ethical systems hashed and rehashed for them *ad nauseam*, continuing to be the rascals they had always been, a little less cruel perhaps, but certainly more hypocritical? Find a way to change tastes, desires, the inner values of the mind, and virtuous conduct will result normally, naturally, without need of sermons, exhortations, laws. Go to the root of the matter, change the character of men, really change it, and the most highly refined system of ethics will instantly become superfluous. Show men how to be spontaneously good instead of boring them with dissertations on virtue!

Even on this road I was going back to my obsession with a spiritual revolution: change in men, change in minds. But I was going to change not only spirits but things as well; in fact, the reason for changing people was to be able to change things more easily and more rapidly. But to change things it was not enough to write their names in books, classify them according to nature and origin, reduce them to general ideas and these generals to universals—eventually establishing the causative relations between the various groups of concepts. It was not enough to exhibit them in show-cases, each show-case labeled with the (inviolable?) law it illustrated. To change reality, it was

jective in view I could not afford to overlook or despise any one. Myth and intuition; image and concept— everything must be put to work. I would exploit every spiritual form in this crusade for the uplifting of the spirit—turning every instinct and every faculty of man toward the creation of a new man.

Chapter 27: Toward a New World

HEAD of a philosophy, its law-giver, apostle, and supreme pontiff! A philosophy of action, a philosophy of doing, of rebuilding, transforming, creating! No more waste of time on unsolvable problems! No more wild goose chasing down roads leading nowhere save into the snares and traps of visionary logicians. The *true* is the *useful*. To *know* is to *do*. Among many uncertain truths, choose the one best calculated to raise the tone of life and promising the most lasting rewards. If something is not true but we wish it were true, we will *make* it true: by *faith*.

A gospel of power, a gospel of courage, a practical, an optimistic, an *American* gospel! Away with fear! Daring! Forward! A leap in the dark! Away with doubt! Every hundred-dollar bill of theory must be convertible into the small change of particular facts, of desirable achievements! Away with metaphysics! Welcome to religions! Metaphysics give the dry concept of the world's outlines; religions open warm and comforting and alluring vistas of lives without end and of values eternally guaranteed at par!

Of what use is a knowledge which in the first place is not knowledge, and which, in the second place, in no way enters our lives nor changes them by one iota? We must have a tool-philosophy, a hammer-and-anvil idea, a theory that produces, a practical promotion and exploitation of spirit!

Taken in this way in a somewhat lyric tone, and duly exaggerated, of course, pragmatism was an inspiration to me. I took the whole movement under my wing, developed it, made it popular, forced it on others, defending, expounding, summarizing it in a rapid fire of books and articles.

But it was not enough for me. It was not sufficiently mine. I had to get it out of the Anglo-Saxon furnished room it had rented from Bible-quoting missionaries in laymen's clothes. I had to set it up in a celestial mansion all its own, a mansion in the Heaven of Absurdity! I either had to make it something truly great or else throw it away.

I adopted therefore that part of pragmatism which promised most—the part which taught how, through faith, beliefs not corresponding to reality could be made *true*. But why limit this action to beliefs? Why create the truth of a few particular faiths only? The spirit should be master of everything. The power of the will should have no limitations whatever! Just as scientific knowledge in a sense creates *facts*, and just as the will to believe creates *truth*, even so the spirit must dominate the all, create and transform at pleasure, *without intermediaries*. So far, to control external things, we have had to use other external things: our minds control our muscles, and these in turn set other parts of material reality in motion before we can move, or change, the reality we have in view. Whereas I wanted spirit to do everything all by itself, by its own fiat, without any go-betweens. Spirit, too, I thought, is one of the forces of nature—in fact, is the noblest, the most perfect, the most refined of them all. Why not the most powerful then? All we have to do is understand, manipulate it. Just as we can already act directly on certain parts of reality (those parts which are parts of our body or are most directly concerned with our lives), so we should be able to act on all of reality in its entirety, without exception. Study and practice should suffice, if only we desire, hope, and try with all our might. If we are victorious all the world will be ours, like a paste, a clay, that can be molded and formed according to our desires. And the prophecy of the First Serpent will be fulfilled: Ye shall be like unto gods!

To be gods! All men—gods! Lo, the dream of dreams, the Emprise Impossible, the long-sought Goal of Glory! It became my program, my platform, for myself and for others: the Imitation of God—Omniscience and Omnipotence, to be attained by way of a Spirit perfected, enlarged, gigantified, endowed with new qualities and new faculties.

Great, in very deed, my dream; but I did not despair of realizing it. Had a man ever before set out deliberately to become God? Men had tried to be charlatans, yes; prophets and miracle workers, yes;—but not gods. Some of them were mistaken for gods, but after their own times and by other people. Divinity was not their goal of attainment but rather an effect of

Chapter 28: The Approach to Divinity

Now indeed, intelligence and goodness, poetry and system, would not help me much!

Before crossing the Atlantic as a prophet of the New Kingdom I would have to *be*—really, effectively *be*—what, during my long vigil, I had dreamed of being and asked others to be: saint, leader, demigod!

The time for plans, hopes, promises, programs, pipe dreams, was past, with some to spare!

Who would have any use for a saint who could not produce his miracle, for a founder without divine prestige, for a god without a god's powers? If that and only that was to be the sole object of my life, I must come to the point without further delay. The divine butterfly must burst from its drab cocoon. The fruit must ripen in fulfilment of the rash promises of the blossoms. I must leap all obstacles, cancel all postponements, burn my bridges, change my life, my character, my soul, seal with action the long-winded advertisement of my intentions!

I did not cajole myself with the confidence that I could do everything all by myself, with nothing to start with. In spite of my haughty scorn of the past, I too would have to attach myself to some tradition, trust myself to the teachings of others, reap the benefit of past experience. Which way was I to turn with the greatest prospect of assistance?

the superstitions prevailing around and after them. The Emperors of Rome, lazy lunatics that they were, believed themselves to be gods; but they thought they were gods already; they did not try to become such. I was different! I wanted to become a god, but I realized that I was still far from being one.

There have been men who proposed to lose themselves in God—mystics, ascetics, saints—but in the sense of reëntering into God, a particle, a drop, an atom of an infinite Deity which creates and integrates, exhales and reinhales (in a rhythmic pant, as it were) all men and all things.

My idea was to be, not a part, but the whole—not a part, but the whole of which everything would be a part—everything obedient to me; as if the mountains, and the stars, and the whirling worlds were members of my body—obedient members. I did not believe in God. God did not exist for me at that time, nor had He ever existed for me. I wanted to create Him for future use and make of myself, a poor, weak, wretched man, a supreme and sovereign Being, all-rich and all-powerful.

I thought of founding a religion on my expectation and preparation of the God-Man. Where? Certainly not in Europe, penniless, intimidated, disillusioned under its crusts of successive civilizations. In America! In that vast North America, with its limitless possibilities, where everything new is welcomed, where every creed finds a temple, and every Moses a capital. I had found a companion quite worthy of me, as crazy as I was, determined to go with me and to share with me the insults and the triumphs in store.

We had thought of everything: of learning English; of studying conditions in North America; of getting the funds we would need to start with. We agreed to spend some years in preparation, living in solitude, studying the question of the power of the mind, experimenting, strengthening our wills, discovering the secrets of direct spiritual action, so as ultimately to be ready to produce miracles and wonders—if the men out there, stubborn as Peters and incredulous as doubting Thomases, asked for them. We even went so far as to choose the name of our new church and to write out the creed of our magic and marvelous faith.

The two of us, two Italians, poor, and philosophers to boot, would go out there to offer to all men omnipotence, wealth, skill, salvation, eternity—everything, in short, which men most ardently desire and crave. The two of us alone would cross the sea to transform that world which an obstinate and unscrupulous Italian had discovered long years before. Thence we would return to Europe, with halos of glory about our heads, followed by thousands of faithful believers, and certain that, propped on this splinter of matter lost in space, we could challenge all other worlds at last made subject to our wills!

The rest would be easy—a mere question of will, of persistence. Once I found the road, progress along it would not be difficult. Where others had gone I too could go!

The saints took me toward religions; the magicians to the occult sciences—roads that diverge only in appearance: religion and magic were born together in the early ages. The saints themselves were miracle workers (even Christ himself?), and the magicians (the real ones) led, as they had to lead, pure, noble, ascetic lives, lives of renunciation and self-sacrifice. I was already well acquainted with both these roads: the heavenly road that went up and up to a consecrated paradise; the underground road that led down and down to hells accursed.

After the failure of my *Aufklärung* I had gone back toward the faiths again with a considerable degree of interest—especially toward Christianity, toward Catholicism. I had re-read the Gospels without the captious Voltairian animosity of my earlier years; I had revisited the churches and cathedrals, not, as before, to admire the architecture, the pictures of the altars and the frescoes in the chapels. I had re-read the Gospels to find Christ; I had reëntered the churches to find God.

Worship attracted me—and not just for the music of the high masses and the beauty of the ceremonial. A vague indefinite something—a curious hunger for believing, for becoming a child again, for feeling myself in communion with the brotherhood I had left—was stirring gently within me, not ready as yet to define itself. I read Saint Augustine; I thought deeply over Pascal; I delighted in the "Little Flowers of Saint Francis." I went as far as the *Introduction à la Vie Dévote* and the "Spiritual Exercises" of the Church. What was it? Psychological curiosity? A desire for information?

To a great extent, yes. But in it also was a grain of the will to believe, a humble desire to have a part in that magnificent religious experiment which from the time of Jesus had been giving the world so many masterpieces of talent and of character. Apologetics interested me; and mysticism, through the examples offered by friends of mine, had a special fascination. I began to hobnob with ancient and modern mystics from Plotinus to Novalis; above all, with the Germans (Meister Eckhart, Suso, Böhme) and the Spaniards (Raymond Lully, Saint Theresa, Saint John of the Cross); both the speculative and the sensuous —not forgetting the hermits or the anchorites, desperate lovers of God, who spent their lives in unceasing prayer in mountain fastnesses. In each of them I found something that seemed to fit my case: exaltation, submersion, immersion in Being, despair, surrender, expectations of the highest destinies.

In some of the heterodox mystics, such as Novalis, I found most explicit promises of what I was looking for, though nothing more than promises, expectations. The others took me up toward the rarefied atmospheres of the most abstract love. But these men asked me to give up my mind, my consciousness, my individuality. They invited me to absorption, to fusion, in the infinite indefiniteness of the one invisible God—not in the ever-flowing, ever-turbulent ocean of the particular. True, some of them, losing themselves in this indefinable, ineffable Deity, had succeeded in doing what I wanted to do: miracles. By renouncing everything, even themselves, even their individualities, they had gained everything. He who loseth his life shall save it! To him who giveth his all shall all be given! Here was a peep-hole on the secret of divine power— but a little one, a very narrow and doubtful one, at best!

In working out a theory of the diversity of being, I had already come to the conclusion that to force the obedience of the All it is necessary to become one with the All. So long as we consider ourselves as *separate* we have no right to give orders to something we do not feel as one with us; and if we give such orders they will not be obeyed. Mysticism, in fact, was a breaking down of barriers, a denial of separateness, an impulse toward absolute and eternal inseparability. The mystic does not feel himself as something apart from the world, from Being, from God. So then, having become an intimate, essential, integral part of the world, every part of his will, no matter how small, is reflected in being. Abdicating as a particular, individual will, he becomes, unconsciously, a sort of universal will; and the most rigorous physical laws fall before the loving desire of an ecstatic.

But even the power of the saints is limited and intermittent, and inherent in the very manner of its attainment is the germ of its unattainableness. Absolute power can be attained only through absolute renunciation of one's Self. But when this complete renunciation has taken place, every memory of thought, every trace of will, every stimulus of desire, will have disappeared, never to return again. In such circumstances volition would be inconceivable and impossible. A person achieving this supreme power would for that very reason be unable to make use of it.

But I, for my part, could never consent to giving up my individuality. Of what use would a complete power be if it were lost in unconsciousness? What I wanted was to exert my power on particular things; to know things, use things, foresee things. No loss of personality for me! No abolition of thought!

So I went off boldly down the other road—toward occultism.

This was not the first time I had attempted to penetrate the outer halls of the accursed temple. In the latter days of my adventures in encyclopedism I had knocked at that same door. The marvelous had always lured me (O wondrous "Arabian Nights," masterpiece of poetic masterpieces!); and it was not even yet beneath me to indulge that appetite in table tipping and in listening to the jumbled words of mediums not oversubtle. In my journeys along the vulgar highways of spiritualism (ridiculous "evening parties," hysteri-

cal old women in black crêpe, red lanterns, nudges with
hands and legs under the tables, suppressed giggles,
painful silences, agonized suspenses, waiting for the
fateful taps to come) I had scraped quite an acquaintance among these spies on the Hereafter. A few of
them, the deepest in their dotage, wanted only to be
convinced that life continued after death. Others,
idealists, aspired to a moral regeneration of this world
through a knowledge of the laws of the next. Still
others, bigger heroes or bigger frauds, I don't know
which, gave to understand that all these little physical
phenomena of mediumism, all these rigmaroles and
abracadabras of Theosophy were nothing, or at most
a mere beginning. They hinted at higher doctrines,
secret traditions, masters invisible or far away, esotericisms of the highest order, reserved for those only who
could survive a thousand terrible tests; and these held
out a promise, couched in vague ambiguous terms, of
power—the very power I was looking for everywhere.
I talked at length with some of them. I read the turgid
source-books of their parasitic wisdom; I attended
several meetings of diabolical shade. I embarked,
gingerly, on a novitiate in Theosophy. I experimented
with the breathing exercises recommended by various
Indo-Yankee Yogees. Insistently I demanded, I
begged, to know their various secrets and offered myself as their disciple. Not that I had any great faith
in all their hodge-podge of theology and symbolism,
from which, according to them, light would eventually

spurt—the light which was to give us new life, a life rich in *powers*. But I did believe that there might be a certain amount of truth in the suggestions offered to disciples so far as they concerned preparation for a mental (and physical) régime different from the usual ones.

At such muddled and chaotic "philosophies," at the ceremonies and the formulas which one generation of charlatans stupidly copied or inherited from the one before it, I could only smile. And yet I was obstinate in my conviction that among all that mass of teachings and experiments, which had been transmitted and tried out over dozens of centuries, between Orient and Occident, there must be something sound, something reliable—the nucleus, perhaps, the seed, the first glimmer of an art of miracle-working.

With my usual fervor I plunged into research, reading, and meditation. Material effects of spiritual causes actually existed, unless all the mediums and medium-followers who ever lived were liars. Telepathy already foreshadowed what future relationships between men might be after slow and heavy intermediaries had been suppressed—the transference of objects to considerable distances, the so-called "materializations" (not denied by everybody), the first examples of transcendental possibilities, of direct psychic control over the inanimate world. These miracles were performed only by abnormal people in unusual states of mind: the point was to make them possible to everybody, even under most ordinary conditions.

Often they were involuntary; they must become voluntary. They were few in number; they must become
commonplaces.

I was convinced that to be successful I must pro-
ceed methodically. Who were the people that performed such wonders? Saints, magicians, mediums:
different names for super-potent individuals of dif-
fering beliefs, who produced very similar prodigies.
Hence, I concluded, the secret could not lie in creeds.
The saint steeped in his Catholic theology; the magician in his cabalistic, Alexandrian, or Paracelsian theology; the medium in a spiritualistic theology à la
Allen Kardec, all did, or hoped they would do, or
promised they would do, the very same things. Therefore, the real cause must be found in some fundamental similarity in all these men, who by chance or
in some religious frenzy—and always spasmodically—
manifested their powers. So there we were! Study
these men, study them deeply, minutely, intimately, in
their beliefs, their systems of life, their constitutions,
their dispositions, their abnormalities! Work out the
physiology and the psychology of the Man of Powers!
This done, we could easily derive a method of sub-
limating the will; and men could be artificially edu-
cated and trained so that to each one could be sys-
tematically apportioned his share of divinity.

I was true to my principle: to think of the instrument and not of the theory; to modify and reform
practice rather than change just words and terminologies. My objective and my procedure once clearly

established, I set furiously to work. Psychologies, general and individual, normal and pathological; legends of saints; autobiographies of seers; minutes of séances and catechisms of initiates; treatises on magic and histories of miracle-working—all were grist to my mill. I devoured them all with my old impatient voracity.

I assembled piles and piles of notes. I followed blind leads. I tried experiments. I would think I had found the way at last; I would fail, give up, and start over again. Time was pressing. I was getting older! I had pledged myself to the most solemn undertaking of my life. I *must* discover that secret and master it at all costs—otherwise, kill myself! I lived in perpetual anxiety—my face pale, my eyes staring, my mind in a daze. Fever! My brain refusing finally to work, my head one throbbing, pulsing pain!

I lost consciousness more than once. More often I would lose my way, unable to grasp the significance of things or remember the meaning of words. My friends grew frightened; but I drove them away with harsh words. I would feel I was going to die and would go off into solitude, regarding every one as an enemy. Without saying a word to a living soul I decided I would withdraw from the world. Up there in the high mountains, there closer to the sky, far from the noise and chatter of the city, I would succeed more easily in vanquishing the mystery. My weakness increased and reached a truly alarming stage. Hideous night-

mares haunted me.   Madness was there at my elbow ready to clutch me.   Everything turned blear and gray about me and about my tottering brain so tensely, so painfully straining toward the Impossible.

I went away, alone, for one last experiment, my mad dream raging in my heart!   Either I would come down from the mountains victorious and dreadful as a god—or I would never come back at all.

However—I came back. . . .

"And below are the vultures that feast on hearts ever renewed."
MATTEO PALMIERI.

Chapter 29: I Come Down from the Mountains

I CAME back again. . . .

I cannot bear to think of that journey home. I cannot tell what it meant in my life. A hideous blush of shame rises to my cheeks. A cold shiver runs down my back. My eyes grow dim. My teeth chatter. My heart seems about to stop beating,—but then it starts going again with a noisy thumping, as though it were trying to silence the inner voice of my remorse.

It was not a return; it was a defeat, a flight, a rout —it was an end.

I felt that the best of my life had been lived; that the part I was to play in the world was closing—there. I should continue, of course, to eat, to sleep, to write, possibly even to achieve "success," to give a little pleasure to people (amusing them with my writings, making a name for myself); but my metaphysical life had been stopped short. It was the end, not of a period, but of a human being, not of an experience, but of a soul.

Hope, pride, perfection, divinity! O dreams so truly dreamed! O enthusiasms so sincerely experienced! O loves insatiate, impatient, like Springtimes too early hot with summer suns! Those of you who have not suffered thus, who have not spent long nights in darkness, waiting for doors to open and a great light to break; those of you who have never pressed parched lips to a cooling fountain; any of you who has not felt himself great on a great mountain top—rival of God, master of men, lord of the earth, above and beyond good and evil, above and beyond the useful and the useless, the small and the great, the base and the noble, alone with himself, alone in Heaven, cannot understand what I felt, what I still feel, as I think of that catabasis.

I came down—down from the heights, down from the mountains, down from the hills. Not as the proud shepherd of the burning bush, with the Laws of Truth graven in his heart and on a stone! Not as the gentle Shepherd from the Mount of Olives to a torture that promised immortality, to a death that would be the beginning of Life. I came down, alone and blind. It was not a descent—it was a fall, a plunge, a crash! Not one smile of hope brightened my face. All was over! Again the mediocrity, the commonplace, the low, the cheap, the insignificant—and *forever*. Farewell to youth! Farewell to divinity! Farewell to *real* life!

I had gone up to the mountains stupidly thinking that three or five thousand feet above the level of the sea I would be nearer heaven. I had shut myself off in solitude, with the notion that outside and beyond the solitude which the strong spirit creates by withdrawing into itself, there was yet another. Resting my head on the close cropped grass of highland pastures, my arms outstretched like a crucified Titan, seeing nothing but the heavenly Infinite of poetry and faith, alone with the open sky, trembling when the stars began to tremble in the deep blue of the twilight, I awaited the moment, the instant when, in an explosion, in a burst of light, the blinding revelation, the miracle would come.

But it did not come! I called, and no one answered my call. I watched and waited; and no one came to me in my suspense. Nature was deaf to my voice. Nothing changed. Everything was just as it had been before. No human being was near me; but I could hear them sneering far away down there on the plains. I could hear them laughing in mockery, pleased, satisfied, delighted at my failure. "And he thought that he could be greater than we are! He thought he could get above humanity! He actually pitied us! And now, look at him! If he wants to get a living, he also must . . . "—A woman, just a woman, was the only one that wept, down there on the plains. Was she really sorry for me? Were her tears sincere? Or was is just a case of wounded vanity?

I fell sick. What little strength I had left deserted me. I returned to town, to my own house, to relatives, neighbors, strangers. I returned as a convict, who for a brief hour thought he had been pardoned, might return to his cell among fellow prisoners. I was not what I had been before. I was not what I had tried to be. I was a monster—an unhappy, ungainly monster. Pale, weak, bashful, self-conscious, I fled from everybody. Nothing in the world of common values could now attract me. Even my friends I shunned. I said I would see no one; that for some time I wished to remain alone, savagely alone, as in the days of my boyhood. I locked myself in my house. I went to another city. I did no work whatever. I answered no letters. I replied to no insults. I requited no love.

What indeed could grip me, hold me, after what I had tried and failed to do? Art? Fame? Thought? Were they not the joys I had left behind, the happiness I had renounced, the goals I had passed without attaining them—because they seemed too obvious, too small, too easy?

How can a man who has desired everything be content with a little? How can the man who has sought heaven be satisfied with the earth? How can the man who has trodden the pathways of divinity be resigned to mere humanity? Impossible! For him everything is closed, lost—over! Beyond help, beyond recall! Nothing more can be done about it! Consolation? Not even that! Tears? But to weep one must have some strength at least; to weep one must have some hope! I am nothing, now! I know nothing. I count for nothing. There is nothing I would lift a finger for nor move a foot for. I am a thing, not a man. Touch me! I am as cold as a stone, as cold as a sepulcher. *Hic jacet!* Here lies a man, who *tried to be God*— and failed!

Chapter 30: I Have Only Myself to Blame

I DO not bawl at you, O Destiny, eternal and abstract Cyrenian of human anemia. Nor do I bear a grudge against the asininity and wickedness of men, who hindered the flowering and fruition of my spirit and did not vouchsafe me the triumphs which I deserved—perhaps!

Yes, friend, notice! I say *perhaps!* I may have been weak: let us therefore not be unjust. God grant me the supreme courage to look with opened eyes into my opened eyes, to read, without halts, pauses, parentheses, reticences, in the book of my memory, to probe, to sound, the depths of its wounds, unmindful of the proud flesh, unmindful of the agony!

I did not succeed in what I had planned. I did not fulfil my promise. I did not attain that high estate of spirit, that glory, that potency which I dreamed of, desired, willed, in the years that are past. Where lay the blame? On those promises, projects, desires themselves—aspirations too great? Not at all! No heights are too high! But our wings are too short, our powers too limited! I aimed at some of those things which are said to be impossible, things which no man has ever accomplished so far in this world. But was not that the very cause of my pride and of my madness? Had I not of my own deliberate choice, voluntarily, gaily, presumptuously, joined that little band of men who seek the impossible because it is impossible, and the undoable because it is undoable!

No! No whining! No alibis! I shall not allege insuperable obstacles, poverty, the mediocrity of my times, the envy of those who knew me, the scorn of those who knew me not, the indifference of most people! Nonsense, such excuses! There is no force so great that it cannot be overcome by a greater force; there is no enemy so strong that he cannot be laid low by a stronger man; there is no poverty so poor as to exclude the possibility of wondrous riches; there is no ice that cannot be melted, warmed, and brought to a boil.

When a man starts out on an enterprise he should take into account all that will be needed to carry it through. If his strength and means are not sufficient, he should either get them before he sets to work or else—give up, go off and hide in a dark corner where he can do what everybody else is doing.

No, my friend, not even that defense will do. The trouble—I can say it now—is this: the weakest men are the men who attempt the biggest things. The greatest cowards try the most foolhardy bravados. It is the hollow chests and the spindly legs that dream of Marathons! Why? More reasons than one! The love of contrariness present in all human affairs. Our need of keeping our courage up, by stimulating, astounding ourselves, with pretensions of power and greatness. Our subconscious thought that we can always excuse ourselves, in the hour of failure, by pointing to the mightiness of what we tried to do. So, pretending to do wonders all the time, we do less than others do, meantime having the satisfaction of grand and glorious defeats! "Poor boy! He had such great ideals! Who knows what he might have done had he been just a little less ambitious!"

All these tricks and traps and subterfuges in the minds of failures I know so well that I have no use for them whatever. Let it never be said that I seek my alibi in a play on words, that I rouge up my poverty of spirit under a cosmetic of poetry and pathos.

I did not succeed because I lacked the brains to succeed, because I did not seriously try to succeed! That is the simple and unadorned truth. I did not succeed because I lacked the necessary strength; because I lacked even the real desire to find or to create the resources I required; because never at every moment in my life did I really have within me, as the axis of my life, as the central dynamo of my soul, the vision which I talked about and glorified in words.

You think it costs me nothing to make this blunt confession of the weakness and the sham in my life? But why should I go on deceiving myself and others?

Oftentimes, instead of keeping to my room with my thoughts alone for company, I would succumb to a moment's impatience and run out into the streets. There I would stop and look at the shop windows, or follow the line of electric lights flaming above my head, or board a clanging, bumping street car, or enter a café to study the illustrations in some low-brow magazine, or go and see my friends to chatter in a stupid, light, or witty conversation with them; or make a social call and drink a cup of coffee out of cup and saucer of gold, flirting with girls from "out of town" or gossiping with affectionate old ladies.

Far too often I would drop a half-finished page at a difficult point to throw myself on my sofa and read any book at all that would make me feel I was think-ing for myself. At such times I even went so far as to look for the jokes in the newspapers. Laziness, sweet and poisonous laziness, with its hundred faces and its hundred smiles, has almost always had its mis-leading, seducing, corrupting charm for me. I would be cold or sleepy; there was not paper enough or pens —any excuse was good to keep me from working! My laziness has postponed, retarded for years and years the radical cure of my mind—power to make a final decision! Besides, I was ever yielding to my body—stomach and sensuality! I have eaten so much at times that I could do no work for hours; or again I would drink so much that a pleasant state of drunken-ness would come over me in which nothing seemed serious, and everything was easy, joyful, far away. I have wasted hours and hours, days and days, nights and nights, with women.

Then again, fear of ridicule often stopped me half way when I was about to compromise myself before the world of belly and pocketbook. Consideration for others, the easy prudence of the World of Get-There, made me timid, uncertain, lukewarm, forgetful. My personal interests, my need of money not infrequently deflected my small remnant of strength from its higher purposes, clouded my mind, forced it to lies, compromises, retreats. Little by little the beautiful hours of exaltation became rarer. New cares took possession of my mind. Sloth stopped my ears with cotton-wool to deaden the clamor of warning or of remorse. Pleasures of a lower order, aims more commonplace, kept me in that state of indolent, however restless, dreaming—the death of all activity—in which I still kept on making promises in words, but in which the great strength of will that I glimpsed in myself at times, all my old enthusiasms and energy, evaporated, died out, leaving only dying embers in my soul glowing now and then under dead gray ashes.

So step by step I came to a frank realization of my impotence. I cast aside my divine plans and my heroic vows that I might write the serious and sorry tale of a mind's defeat. I have only myself to blame. And I do blame only myself—in the hope perhaps that frankness will win pardon for a little of my past cowardice.

Chapter 31: Days of Shame

I BELIEVE that I am often one of the most hypocritical time-wasters in this world.

I sleep ten consecutive hours without waking, without dreaming. When I get up my head is heavy, my tongue thick. I go out-of-doors with nothing in view. I come home to rest. I eat voraciously. I sip a large cup of coffee. I smoke five or ten cigarettes. I lounge in one armchair and put my feet on another. I read the newspaper from end to end like a pensioned civil service official. I go out to meet some acquaintance of a skeptical turn of mind for a round or two of verbal sparring, ironical, bitter, stupid. I enter a café, drink a cup of corn-starched chocolate, and get away with three or four disgusting vanilla éclairs. I run through a bundle of crumpled and torn periodicals and almost smile as I squint at the idiotic cartoons in color. Again I go out into the street now ablaze with the theater lights. I follow a painted and powdered prostitute as if she were a first love. I drop into a bookshop and for a few cents buy a book with uncut pages which I will never read. I stop in front of a grocer's window and hungrily look at the greasy cheeses and the boxes of sardines. I call at a house where I am welcome for tea, and I drink four, five, six cups, hoping it will help me get back a little of my brains. If I feel like it—and even if I don't—I step into a brothel to kill time, a few minutes, a few hours, to forget the things which I should be doing and am not doing, to degrade myself, to debase myself, to stifle my remorse, to drug my conscience. Every now and then, when I cannot help myself, I write a letter or even ten letters, to get rid of them, to get rid of everybody, all at once; and occasionally, in the evening, when my heart is really too full and I am inconsolably unhappy I take my big black pen in hand and write down anything that comes into my head. Madly I cover ten, twenty, forty sheets of white paper with my explosions of emotion, my expressions of contrition, my strained, witty, rarefied, and distilled absurdities.

But what can you expect of a man who divides his time between slumber and coffee, between table and bed, lazy, sleepy—good at blowing the trumpet, not so good when it comes to fighting the battle he has called for? I rise in my wrath from warm sheets or over-stuffed armchairs to scream like an eagle because my spirit is insulted; and I lay out a plan for an austere, solitary, scornful, noble life—something in the style of Michelangelo—for my fellow men to live.

Let no one say I do not feel the infamy of this double life I lead. I do feel it; and the more deeply I feel it the more deeply I wallow in it to forget my shame. Confession comforts me a little. But when I have mirrored the lurid picture of a self-betrayer in angry words that all may see it and spit upon it, I imagine I am forgiven, saved. I arise with an air of

triumph, as if this disgusting exhibitionism had purified and transformed me. The next day I continue as
before. I go to bed at nine o'clock. I sleep ten
hours without waking or dreaming. I get up with an
empty head and with a bitter taste in my mouth; and
I spend the day in the self-same manner I confessed
to with shudders the day before. And again, alas,
when I can no longer bear it, I sit down at my table
and again begin to spoil another ream of paper with
words, words, words, singing in verses of countless syl-
lables the miseries of the ascetic hero who sees human
things with divine eyes!

So low have I fallen that never once do I think of
dropping arsenic into the cup of yellow, over-sweet-
ened tea I have at my elbow.

Chapter 32: What Do You Want of Me?

AND yet everybody wants to see me. Everybody insists on having a talk with me. People pester me and they pester others with inquiries about what I am doing. How am I? Am I quite well again? Is my appetite good? Do I still go for my walks in the country? Am I working? Have I finished my book? Will I begin another soon?

A skinny monkey of a German wants to translate my works. A wild-eyed Russian girl wants me to write an account of my life for her. An American lady wants the *very latest* news about me. An American gentleman will send his carriage to take me to dinner —just an intimate, confidential talk, you know. An old schoolmate and chum of mine, of ten years ago, wants me to read him all that I write as fast as I write it. A painter friend I know expects me to pose for him by the hour. A newspaper man wants my present address. An acquaintance, a mystic, inquires about the state of my soul; another, more practical, about the state of my pocketbook. The president of my club wonders if I will make a speech for the boys! A lady, spiritually inclined, hopes I will come to her house for tea as often as possible. She wants to have my opinion of Jesus Christ, and—what do I think of that new medium? . . .

Great God, what have I turned into! What right have you people to clutter up my life, steal my time, probe my soul, suckle my thoughts, have me for your companion, confidant, and information bureau? What do you take me for? Am I an entertainer on salary, required every evening to play an intellectual farce under your stupid noses? Am I a slave, bought and paid for, to crawl on my belly in front of you idlers and lay at your feet all that I do and all that I know? Am I a wench in a brothel who is called upon to lift her skirts or take off her chemise at the bidding of the first man in a tailored suit who comes along?

I am a man who would live an heroic life and make the world more endurable in his own sight. If, in some moment of weakness, of relaxation, of need, I blow off steam—a bit of red hot rage cooled off in words—a passionate dream, wrapped and tied in imagery—well —take it or leave it—but *don't bother me!*

I am a free man—and I need my freedom. I need to be alone. I need to ponder my shame and my despair in seclusion; I need the sunshine and the paving stones of the streets without companions, without conversation, face to face with myself, with only the music of my heart for company. What do you want of me? When I have something to say, I put it in print. When I have something to give, I give it. Your prying curiosity turns my stomach! Your compliments humiliate me! You tea poisons me! I owe nothing to any one. I would be responsible to God alone—if He existed!

Chapter 33: Glory

AND even if I were to succeed—even if I could throw into your faces—you who have despised, tortured, mocked, reviled, ridiculed, persecuted, ignored me— the great work I have dreamed of and longed for, the masterpiece that would bring tears to your dry stingy eyes, that would close your obscenely leering lips, and give a thrill to those sodden peewee hearts of yours (which even you have forgotten you have somewhere down under your shirt-fronts), if I could in short defeat, vanquish, overwhelm, confound you with a blinding flash of genius—what could you give or offer me in exchange, in what way could you think of rewarding me?

The history of human sorrow is the history of your gratitude and recognition! A fine thing, this glory of yours, I must say!

Imagine! I give you the best of myself—shreds of my living flesh, drops of my heart's blood, the innermost secrets of my life! And what do you give me? Publicity! Nothing else? You review me in your newspapers without understanding what I write. You bore me with visits and letters. You point at me when I go out for a walk or take a seat in a café or in a theater. You force me to write on order, when I have nothing to say, when all I can do is repeat myself. You worry me for letters, opinions, autographs, articles. You watch—and then you tell—where I go, whom I go with, what I do when I get there. You stick up my ugly picture everywhere, in books, in newspapers, on street corners, on postcards. Then at last when I am dead, you rummage through my papers, make public property of the intimacies of my life, haul out the rags and rubbish of my biography, and finally erect an ugly effigy of me in marble or bronze in some public square! This is what you offer me!

Ah, yes! Vanity is mighty, even in the great—I know that. But are there not sensitive souls as well? Are there not also spirits who feel they are solely and purely spirit, who are offended and sullied by all this adoration of boneheads? What counts in me—if I have anything that counts—is my soul. Why photograph, why paint, why perpetuate, my body then? If I am great it is because I have had the strength to live by myself. Why then do you herd about me upsetting me with your smells and your stares? If I have given you any object lesson, it has been that the greatest thing a man can do is to add nature to Nature, life to Life, mind to Mind, and not nibble, gnaw, remasticate the words of others. Why then do you waste your time trying to explain what I have said instead of feeling an impulse to surpass me, destroy me, with something better of your own?

If what I have said is well said, why say it over worse? If a person does not understand me, do you think you can explain me to him? Do you think you can explain my words just as I wrote them—designing them, engraving them, each and every one, on my most effervescent nights of inspiration?

Oh, of course, these complaints are ridiculous, especially in my mouth. Why seek outside yourself the recompense you have within you? If the creation of your work, the lives of the people born of you, the richness of the imagery you invented, are not enough to make you satisfied and happy, what do you think men can do for you? Can they, the small, the cold, the mediocre, give you something your genius could not give you? Do your work without thinking of them! Throw your creations at people to terrify or comfort them,—but then go on creating as long as your strength endures! Are you a bricklayer, waiting for a pay envelope every Saturday night when the work is done? Yours are not houses of stone and plaster, but mansions of words and blood—neither glory nor money can pay for them.

Neither glory nor money—but the sorrow that is sweet, the glory that is silent! These, yes!

Oh, if only I could be really close to those few—be they but three, or four, or seven, or ten—who read with their whole souls and not with just their eyes, who live with an author and love him as a brother, though they have never seen him; who dream of him, and speak of him to each other on melancholy Sunday walks, nourished by his thoughts, intoxicated by his poetry, trembling for his welfare, waiting for a word from him as prophets await revelation from God—

then, yes, then I would be happy; then I would feel truly compensated for the silence of the past and the insipid stupid clamor of the present! If only I could clasp you to my heart—pale, sad, disconsolate soul who were the first to read and love my writings—you to whom I, alone and before all others, disclosed the bitter taste of greatness and the feverish joy of poetry! One of your smiles, a quickened beating of your heart, a long and happy gaze from your eyes, one of your restless dreams, would be a sweeter and more precious gift to me than all the parrot chatter of the mobs, all the golden wreaths that are flung at me. I do not want applause, hurrahs, open mouths, forced praises, envious adulation! No! No! None of your "sensations," none of your "furors" for me! Keep your brass bands and bass drums, your sopranos, your dancers, and your fat tenors for yourselves. Keep your acorns for swine, if you have no pearls for heroes!

Chapter 34: And Supposing—

AND supposing I had acquired powers? Supposing I had become a kind of earthly demigod, lord of heaven and earth, conqueror of matter and death, master of men and of minds? What would I have done with my powers? To what use would I have put my sovereignty over the universe?

During my mystical straining for a much-hoped-for "control," I hardly ever thought of the afterwards. I was pursuing "means" without knowing the "ends" to which I would use them. I wanted to be God, regardless of the fact of my creation and regardless of the law governing *my* being. The world was already created: well and good! But its law was such that at a touch from man everything would fall apart, go to pieces. Yes, but then what?

Able to do *everything*—absolutely *everything!* But do what? It is impossible to act without first making a choice. But how could I choose when the possibilities of choosing were infinite in number? Choice implies preference—this rather than that, a purpose, an objective, a heart-yearning toward an ideal believed in. Thus fortified, I could annihilate whatever I despised, perpetuate whatever I loved, direct the course of things toward my own goal, model my ideal in the responsive clay of the actual.

But I had none of these—neither loves, nor aims, nor dreams. *Power* was my only love, *power* my only aim, *power* my highest dream. But *after* power, what? I was empty—I felt as empty as a well that seems to be bottomless only because it reflects the far-away depths of the sky.

Do what? The answer is difficult enough, even for the barely superior man, hemmed in on all sides by impossibilities and limitations. He knows he cannot take this road and that road; but the one that is left is shorter and safer. The man for whom there are no walls, no barriers, no restrictions anywhere, who is theoretically free, theoretically omnipotent, finds the question "what to do?" a thousand times more enigmatic and dangerous.

Do what? For a mere exercise of powers, one thing is as good as another. When a man rises so high that he no longer has the needs, interests, loves, truths of a human being, everything is on the same plane. The destruction of a race, the creating of a new species, have the same value and significance. To give happiness to a beggar or reduce an epicure to poverty are, on that high level, one and the same thing. Justice and injustice, the high and the low, are meaningless distinctions. The moment human values rise above the sphere of humanity they blend and disappear. The sentiments a man feels are all products of his impotence. Let him acquire absolute power, and he is dehumanized, superhumanized, yes,—but he becomes insensible, a lifeless thing lacking in resilience, will, direction.

Dead level: a bird's nest and a metropolis; a grain of sand and a peninsula; a fool and a genius—all equally respectable, all equally ridiculous! Why should I care more for one part of reality than for another, if it's *all* mine, all at my disposal, all under my control?

A great part of the pleasure we derive from doing (changing or possessing) something depends on the effort we expend in doing it. "How splendid, how strong I am! No one else could have done what I have done!" After all our trouble in getting it, the object of our desire, though it be a worthless trifle—a woman, a house, an instant of fame—takes on an inordinate value for us: it becomes a consoling prize won by the triumphant sweat of our brow. But if ability to do involved no fatigue, if an exertion of the will, the whispering of a command, the winking of an eye, is enough to exact the immediate and unlimited obedience of all things, where is the victory? What is the fun?

So I think I am lucky on the whole that I did not get to be a god, in the stupid, literal way I thought of. I would have been unhappier than I am. And perhaps the knowledge that I was *able* to do all things would have satisfied me, and I would have done nothing. I would have remained motionless and unmoved for ever —powerless from too much power. And I should desperately have mourned the anxious days of hoping and waiting that I had lost, days when I could still will and choose and pursue an objective.

But all this talk, again! Is it nothing but a post-humous consolation for a great failure? What a dog a man is! O Adam, kicked out like a thief before you have passed the garden gate, you now deny the savor and the perfume of the fruit you never tasted?

Chapter 35: Am I a Fool?

ALL of my life has been based on the belief that I am a man of genius. But what if I were mistaken? What if I were one of the many blind who mistake reminiscences for inspirations, desires for achievements? What, in a word, if I were a fool?

Would that be so strange?

Would that be the first time a simpleton has imagined himself a hero, a man of letters a poet, an idiot a great man? Is it not possible, a thousand times possible, that I am nothing but a frigid reader of books, warmed from time to time by the fires others have kindled; witty with the wit of others; mistaking the sluggish murmuring of an ambitious mind for the gurgling of a full spring ready to burst the rock, water the thirsty earth, and reflect the blue sky?

The more I think of it the more possible, probable, natural, it seems to me. What gives me the right to believe in myself and in my genius? My achievements? But I am the first to deny and scorn them! What are my writings but dishwater drained from the literary sinks of all the nations; disordered nightmares of a friendless pervert, tricks of an intellectual acrobat —what else? What else?

My confidence in being a genius lies in a long and futile anticipation of some overwhelming and triumphant inspiration; in my eternal spirit of unrest that nothing satisfies; in my scorn for all but a celestial and Platonic world, which I seem to glimpse at times through the clouds of the real world, in moments of vision that quickly pass; in the slender, tenuous, fleeting moods of poetry, the flashing images so swiftly taking form in words that often pass through my mind when I am thinking without seeing—evenings on my way home across my bridges, above me the sky, beneath me the river, both tremulous with myriad stars.

But what does that prove? Discontent is so often an excuse for the most sallow-faced weakness! The desire for fame is so very common even among down-and-outs! Those brief squalls of imagination never become the tornado that sweeps the world and whirls men up to the angels and to the stars. All those disconnected, disjointed impressions of mine, all those lonesome, homeless idealets, all those squirts of inspiration that are soon plugged again, all those short-lived flashes of wit, all those happy phrases—never ordered, organized, correlated, fused in a supreme masterpiece, in a work of life complete and full—are of no value whatever! They count for nothing. Much more than they will ever be is needed to place a man on equal terms with the great creators, and give him the right to climb the heights and revile or pity the chesty, self-satisfied mortals who are strutting around below. Sparks that fly and die, will-o'-the-wisps that glow and vanish, phosphorescences that flicker and wane, lightning flashes veiled in cloud, lights faint in the distances, flares that rise and fade in a second—these things never make a fire. They are promises, temptations, allurements; they are the kindlings ever renewed of vanity, the meager extenuations of a hell-bound sterility, the agonized convulsions of an aborted fœtus. In them there is no hope. Nay, it were better if they did not exist! These snorts of insignificance are the brands of infamy and torture that mark the halfway man—the man who is neither a perfect beast, nor yet a supreme genius, who is neither a plant that vegetates perennially, nor a mind that furiously creates —who is neither a pudgy bale of merchandise, nor a pillar of fire leading the peoples.

I am a mediocre man—the infamous mediocrity I loathe with all my being. I am that thing which will cease to be any thing when my blood no longer flows, and my lungs expand with their last breath of air. I may have been something once, a long time ago, and for the space of a few minutes. I may have spent all the genius given me in a single night, in a single round of the game I do not know. Here I am now, like a Jew, who has eaten the grapes of the Promised Land on a day of hurried vintage and now finds himself athirst with lips parched in the midst of a sandy desert. I am like a man suspended between heaven and earth, too fat to soar to the skies, too ethereal to wallow in the muck. The dregs of culture, the reminiscences of the poets, the swimming and swarming of thoughts in my head unfit me for the solid life of a practical mechanic; yet they are not enough to make me worthy of membership among the kings of intellect. Oh, that I had never known—even for an instant, even from afar —the impassioned joy of creation! Oh, that I had been born and had remained a gentle, harmless, irresponsible imbecile, a modest simpleton without remorse, a good-natured idiot without pretensions. But no such luck for me! I know I am a fool. I realize I am an idiot—a knowledge and realization that take me out of the class of morons who are happy because they are perfect morons. I am just superior enough to know that I am not superior enough. Possibly with the passing years I shall become a more sodden imbecile. Then if my happiness is no greater, at least my torment will be less. I may hope to turn into a tree or a stone, and to come to rest at last in a beatific state of complete unconsciousness.

Chapter 36: And an Ignoramus

AND then, after all, let us tell the obnoxious truth: I am an ignoramus!

I have rummaged everywhere, I have stirred up everything, I have smelled the perfume and plucked the petals of all the Knowable. I have beaten my head against the stone wall of the Unknowable.

But I have never gone to the bottom of anything.

I cannot truthfully say that I am master of any science, art, or philosophy. I have no specialty, I have no "field," which, small though it be—a diminutive garden plot—I can call my *own,* in which I can look down on any one who gets under my feet.

I may give others, many people in fact, the impression that I am one of those amphibious, castrated, emasculated individuals who are called (with undue disrespect to agriculture) "cultivated men." I have read a book or two, in fact very many, perhaps too many books; and yet I may say that I have never read anything. My mind is filled with an army of names, with a horde of titles; it is a warehouse of notes; but the books I know inside and out, in word and in spirit, the books I have read, re-read, and inwardly lived, are very, very few indeed—and I am ashamed to admit it; though I am not the only unfortunate who has wasted his time writing words in the sand which a gust of wind will wipe out. The famous "man of one book" is a dismal and dangerous customer: but the man of too many books is a cesspool that keeps only the worst of the sewage that comes into it. I am such a man. *Mea culpa!*

I was a born self-teacher; and the self-taught man is great only when he succeeds in maturing and restraining himself. I am the encyclopedist, the man of dictionaries and textbooks; and the encyclopedist is indeed wonderful if he can manage to bind the dried and faded facts of varied readings into sheaves, with the iron bands of fundamental principles.

I can dazzle not a few with my knowledge of bibliography. I can hold my own in a talk with specialists. But in five minutes, or in five days, I have run dry: my pack is emptied. I have other bags at home, but they are not good measure. They are always short by a peck or more, and what is there has not all been sifted.

Whichever way I turn I am not the layman, nor yet am I of the guild. No legitimate chair is accorded me among the learned: I have never been labeled. I am a man without a place; yet I can stay in any spot I choose till they put me out.

A wandering Jew of knowledge, I have settled in no country, I have gained residence in no city. Lashed by the demon of curiosity I have explored rivers and wilds without plan and without patience—always in a hurry, ever on the wing. I have much information but few foundations. I am like a king who rules over a vast empire of maps.

I have begun everything and finished nothing. I am no sooner launched on a certain road than I take the first turn to the right, or to the left, thence branching into by-paths that lead to other by-paths, till I find myself on another highway.

When people marvel at my learning, my erudition, I feel like laughing in their faces. I alone know how many appalling voids there are in my brain. I alone, who have longed to know everything, know how limited the field of my knowledge is. The periods of antiquity, the dead languages of the great nations, the sciences of light, of movement, of life, are almost closed books to me. I know their vocabulary and several of their paragraphs; I have an idea of their whole; but I cannot go ahead on my own legs. I am ignorant, immeasurably, hopelessly ignorant. The worst of it is that mine is not the simple natural ignorance of the woodsman or the farmer, which is not incompatible with freshness and serenity, nor even with a certain canny originality. No, I am just an ignoramus, a fool who has buried himself in books, a library-donkey, who has learned enough to lose all spontaneity, without acquiring any real wisdom.

And yet I have had the impudence to want to be a teacher, to become a professor overnight, to be an "inspirer," and "guide" and "beacon" to others. I have written books with footnotes and bibliographies. I have passed judgment on the monographs of other people. I have given the impression of mastering my subjects, and of knowing what I was talking about. I have attained no mean reputation as a "scholar," a "plodder," a "man who takes notes," who is "well-posted." How great must be the ignorance around me, if I have gotten away with that reputation! I can tell for my part how easily won is that false fame which certain "scholars" wheedle out of a blind and lazy public at so little cost! Knowing the heads and tails of my own "learning," knowing how light, how flimsy the curtain of my erudition is, knowing how meager the preparation behind my cocksureness, how great the timidity underneath my rashness, I am ashamed of myself, I am ashamed of others; and I feel impelled to confess aloud to those who would listen to me.

How can anything good or great come from a man so sunk in the slime of ignorance? Knowledge is Power! What wonder if my power remains—oh, tortured memory, oh, burning remorse—in the ash-can of unrealized desires? And whom shall I blame for this?

Myself, always myself, only myself! If I had been a little weaker (weak enough not to dream), or a little stronger (strong enough to conquer), I would not now be abasing myself before men whom I despise!

Chapter 37: I Do Not Know Men

IGNORANT not only of things, but of men!

What was my life's great plan? To influence my own species, change it fundamentally from beast to man, from man to god, begin a new era in the history of the world, date from me the mystic hejira of humanity.

But to influence men one must know them; to change them one must get inside them with love and sympathy. Without daily and direct contact with all of them—with townsman and rustic, with schoolboy and factory hand, with the woman who hopes and the woman who suffers, with the kings of the earth and the beggars of the gutter—you cannot tear them from life as it is and push them up toward something better. Whosoever would find a way to their hearts, discover the deeper springs of their conduct, must know their most hidden thoughts, their most vital needs, their best secreted choices. We have the man of the scientists whom psychology puts before us in books of three hundred pages, or in definitions of thirty words; we have the man we see about us, a man all exterior, all front, who adapts himself to others on his own account to make a good impression on his fellow men. This man is easily recognized; you can draw his picture with a few strokes of the pen. But the true man, the

real, the concrete man, is not to be found in the philosopher's dummy, nor yet in the disguises worn by our
friends. The apostle, the prophet, the Messiah, must
know the man that hides behind his words and his
make-up. He must know—not man, but men, this man
and that man—thousands of men, individually, one by
one, in all their intimate aspects emotional and mental.

I did not know them; and so I was bound to fail.
If we refuse to listen to people, we cannot expect them
to listen to us. I was a stranger to men and men do
not understand the language of strangers. They cannot love some one who has not a terrible love for them.
Humanity is a woman, drawn only to those who adore
her or frighten her.

For this reason I too tried to know men. I tried
to be much with them, take them by the arm, listen
to what they said, note their involuntary self-revela-
tions.

I was willing to try everything. I visited the poor
in their hovels, to record their indictments of society
at first hand. I stopped by the man with the shovel,
with the plane, with the hammer, to enter into the
spirit of his work, divine his conception of happiness.
I followed strangers along crowded streets, to learn
their mode of life. I even consented to frequent well-
mannered and fashionable people and I shivered with
cold and with rage in their overheated drawing rooms.
I talked with waiters and baggage men. I drew out
children and their mamas. I loitered about churches
and eavesdropped on black-robed women as they raised

their childish prayers to the Madonna. I sought out priests in the rectories and monks in the monasteries. I went to the classrooms of great scholars and to the studios of unknown artists. I studied the ledgers of merchants and exchanged confidences with their clerks. I made harlots tell me stories of their lives. I breathed the heavy air of cheap dives and eating-houses to hear the talk of people I wanted to redeem.

I tried to force my way into the lives of others. I typed with stenographers. I took notes with students. I dissected corpses with surgeons. I made hay with peasants. I drove donkeys with street peddlers. I gossiped at dinner with dukes and marquises. I used the plumbline with bricklayers and wielded the pick-ax with laborers.

And yet it was all in vain. I drew nigh unto you, O men, and yet I do not love you. I cannot love you. You disgust me. You revolt me. Since I did not love you, I could not know you; and not knowing you I could not save you. I was alone in your midst, all to myself; and you left me to myself. So my words now leave you silent, and my promises do not stir you. You were right then. You are right now.

Like all who have tried to change your destinies, I feel conflicting emotions within me. I approach you to know you better; but no sooner do I begin to know you than I am disgusted. To rid myself of this disgust I ought to change you; but I cannot change you, since I know not how you are made. This vicious circle, a girdle of despair, has strangled most reformers in the end. We all have an immense love for humanity when we are alone in our own houses. But let us go out and rub elbows with Peter and Judas, with men who walk and talk and have their being, and our love changes to scorn and hate. We go back to our corners again and, lo, in the desert our love blooms again for all men, even for Peter and Judas.

Such is my case. I love you, O men, as few have loved you. All my inner being is suffused with this deep affection. I would have you bigger, happier, purer, nobler, mightier than you are. My fondest dream has been to be your real, your greatest redeemer.

But mine is a jealous love, a love hidden, strange, bizarre. I try to express it in words and the words freeze on my lips. I open my arms to embrace you and my ardor becomes loathing. I feel the warmth of your breath, and my heart is poisoned. Mine is a love that is mine, peculiarly, intimately my own. It is a lonely, a selfish, an impotent love. It should burn more brightly at sight of my loved one. Instead it dies down, and goes out. It should express itself in loving deeds, in kindly words. Instead it rebukes, it scourges, it reviles. My love is a love of slaps and sputa. You cannot understand, O men, you cannot accept, such love.

In moments like these, in moments of pitiless frankness, I cannot reproach you. The fault is in me, in my coldness, which keeps me from losing myself in you, as a lover melts in his loved one. You sense the mockery in my smile. You see my fist clench as I shake your hand. Thou, too, humanity, art of the violent; and I have not known how to love thee or to chastise thee enough.

I have nothing but intentions without power within me. It is my lot to suffer a self-inflicted torture with no right to ask you for a word of comfort. I am a little Prometheus, harboring the vulture of remorse in my vitals because with the fire I have stolen I can burn only myself.

Chapter 38: Inspiration

Oh, that the deep and majestic stream of inspiration might burst forth in me like a water jet, long and forcibly repressed! Oh, that ideas might spout in me like fantastic fountains mounting to the skies! Oh, that images, and thoughts, and sentiments—and words of blessed finality!—might fall like rain on my heart, and on the hearts of men, cooling, consoling, softening, rousing to fertility! Oh, that my mind might suddenly burst into flame like a field of brushwood and stubble, like a thicket of dry wood. Oh, that my thoughts might illumine the heavens like sputtering rockets; that my words might burn like fire; that ideas might fly from my racing pen like sparks from a smoldering log stirred by the tongs. Oh—and above all—that I might enlighten, and warm, the minds of all men!

Why am I denied this joy, this happiness, this bounty —I, who have asked for it, waited for it, yearned for it, prayed for it?

Oh, if some day, after so many years of impatient waiting, of frantic invocation, I could hear roaring in me a torrent of new words, feel surging over me a wave never felt before! Oh, that, instead of writing the same old things, of stringing together the same old phrases, of crawling along the same old paths with the same old tired and patched-up thoughts, new unexpected truths should rise to my lips—marvelous images, rhythms, harmonies, and passions, as yet undiscovered, unknown, unfelt by any man!

How many times at night, by the red flickering light of a candle, or in the calm white glow of a shaded lamp have I waited for the coming of the divine hour —as, at midnight, the ever-disappointed lover awaits the coming of the girl who has at last promised to be his! And at such times I would tear the white sheets of paper—half covered with scribbles—one after another into bits. I would rub my eyes with my hands and stupidly gaze at some stupid object. Half asleep I would draw profiles of monsters and old men with beards. Then I would destroy more paper. And I would curse myself, jump to my feet, kick back my chair, throw down my pen, and roll about on my bed, unable to sleep, unable to dream, unable to forget.

Thus it was a hundred, a thousand times; my mind remained ever hard and perverse, my soul ever cold and dead, my paper ever white before me—and fame as far away as before. No! Genius had I none. There was no answering echo in the Infinite. Heroic frenzy refused to awaken in me; darkness, silence, torture!

What would I not have done, what would I not do, to be shaken, shocked, aroused for a moment, to receive, suddenly, the mysterious dictation of a Truth revealed!

An inspiration, whether of God or of the Devil, so it be a power greater than I am, saner than I am, more far-seeing, more mad, that speaks through my mouth, writes with my hand, thinks with my thought!

Chapter 39: My Debts

BUT God refuses to speak through my mouth—I shall never write a holy scripture. And the Devil, who is fond of light literature, keeps clawing me down toward a nether Hell of horrors.

But—I am afraid that some one will speak through my mouth all the same. As yet, I do not know myself. I have hacked my spirit into bits, until now my soul is in pieces, shattered, lifeless, its fibers tangled and exposed, like the pictures in books of anatomy. I do not know myself. I do not recognize my own voice. When I am speaking I do not know whether the words come from my own brain or from some hideous prompter crouching behind my back.

I feel I am a *debtor*.

All men are debtors, though few of us admit our debts, and fewer still have any intention of paying them.

The history of the human mind is one long record of protested checks.

Like the savages of the South Sea, we devour our fathers; but we are not always as successful as they in digesting them.

Yet after each feast we recognize the vomit as our own.

I feel infinitely in debt. With Saint Paul I can say:

"I am debtor to the Greeks, and to the Romans, to the Hebrews and to the Gentiles." I could add another half-dozen peoples and still the account would not be closed. I am like the men of the Golden Age—I do not know mine from thine. I have not stolen with the deliberate idea of stealing. I dislike plagiarism—only the very poor and the very rich can indulge in that. I have snuffed at everything, I have absorbed everything that has come under my hand, and now I am unable to divide the goods and tell which is whose. I am steeped in other people's theories. I am stuffed with other people's books, articles, phrases, images. I am a product of others,—whereas I would like to be a genius, and *myself*.

This uncertainty is a torment to me. I would like to know what I really am, to what extent the things I have done are mine. I would like to give to others after having stolen from them. I would like to add something to the civilization that has been my sustenance. I would like to find myself in the general mixture; settle my accounts, get away with my own belongings—though they weigh but an ounce. I put my name under the titles of my books; but I would like to know just what I have borrowed, just what is really mine. I am so completely plastered with other people that I don't know where my own limbs begin. I am singing in a chorus and cannot distinguish the sound of my own voice.

The situation disgusts me. This communism is a bore. This suspicion of theft troubles my conscience.

I prefer to owe no man anything. I would rather do without than have to be grateful to my creditors. I insist upon being *myself*, only myself, individual, independent, without ties, the sole and lawful proprietor of myself and all that belongs to me. I am Robinson Crusoe without an island.

Whereas, at present, when I re-read what I have written, I am always afraid of finding that I have been trespassing on the property of others. That word there—may I not have taken it from such and such an author? This image here—may it not be a reminiscence of another? This idea may be a disguise and a development of some one else's idea. This character may have been suggested to me by some novel, or possibly by some living person. This joke I may have heard in conversation with a friend. The shades of the living and the dead crowd about me; and I would like to throw back at them all their loans— principal and interest alike.

Many people have no such scruples. I envy them.

I do not want to take anything, not even from reality. I wish I were a spider drawing the threads of my work from my own insides. The bee steals its honey from the flowers! How odious! I would like to be indebted to myself and to myself alone.

Not even the skies, the faces of men, the trees of the woods, the houses of the cities, should give me anything. I cannot do without them. And yet I am ashamed to find them in me, in my writings. It saddens me to think that probably I should be unable to say anything without that sky, that face, that tree, that house. I wish I could make a clearing about my mind to see what it can do when it stands all alone. An absurd thought, a ridiculous desire, an impossible undertaking! Forget it! But I cannot help feeling that I am the anti-debtor *par excellence*, anti-debtor to the point of madness.

But there is worse yet! I am afraid at times that I owe even what I may call my talent to entirely extraneous things—material things, into the bargain. My wit is keener after two cups of coffee. I am a better reasoner after a pot of tea. A few glasses of champagne add to my gifts of gay paradox. A climb to a hilltop makes me a more moral man. If a café orchestra, a military band, a movement from a symphony, give me a poetical flight, or suggest thoughts, images, sentences I would not have thought of by myself, I must suspect to my shame that I am only a thinking machine which gives out what is put into it, which cannot work without fuel and oil. I must fear it is not I who think and dream, but the coffee, the tea, the wine, the oxygen, the music that are dreaming and thinking in me. A stupid fear, perhaps! Many people drink and hear what I drink and hear, without ever doing what I do. Never mind! These red and white liquids I pour into my stomach do have an effect on me. Without them I would not think what I think nor write what I write. It angers, it irritates me to realize that these extraneous material substances are parts of my inspiration, collaborators in my work.

To owe something to Shakespeare is a remorse. But to owe more to a ham sandwich is a disgrace.

I do not know how many people suffer this damnable torment of not being able to find themselves in their own personality. The Greeks with their "know thyself," and Ibsen with his "be thyself," trouble me beyond words. How can I know my real self if I cannot identify myself, if I cannot isolate the irreducible center, the ultimate residuum, of my individuality?

I am not looking for man, nor yet for *a* man; I want myself, just my Self! Who is this Self? And where is he? And what does he really think? Yet with this Self, bound, dressed, wrapped, cluttered up by others—I must live, and always live as a stranger.

This—but not only this—is the torture of my hard life.

Chapter 40: The Clown

RATHER than die of hunger and cold like an alley cat, I will take up any trade. I will pick rags in the streets with a pack on my back. I will stand in front of churches and restaurants begging pennies in the name of God. I will be a cleaner in a public latrine. I will lead a dancing bear through country towns. If, really, I can find nothing else to do I will become a lawyer.

But there is one trade I will never follow—no, not even if I am ordered to, with a revolver at my back. I will never be a literary buffoon. I will never be a "clown author." I will never be the man who writes to amuse people, to pass time pleasantly for the bored and the lazy. I will never be a contemptible wretch who from January 1st to January 1st invents stories, manufactures plots, thinks up adventures, rehashes histories, works out novels, writes short stories, rigs up plays to make people who pay and applaud him laugh or cry.

These public mountebanks may prate of beauty, pretend to turn up their noses at the public, hide in their vest pockets the money they get for the fun they provide. It does them no good. They may like it or lump it; but they are prostitutes serving the Sovereign Mob that would forget its shameless day in an evening of pleasure. They are the hired clowns of

the People; jesters and fools to drummers and sales-
men who would snuff a book between puffs of cigar
smoke. A peddler of fiction is a bootblack of the idle
rich. He is a panderer offering the sham life of others
to people who have no life of their own. What is
the difference, in effect, between a cigar and a story,
a drama and a bottle of wine? Smoking and reading
you pass time more easily. A play, like a good drunk,
takes you off into another world where you see things
and dream things that do not exist.

There is, to be sure, one difference: Art. You can,
I grant you, say many beautiful things this way, and
there are books of this kind that may live long in
the hearts of men. But underlying them all is the
notion that men, above everything else, must be
amused and made to laugh—that a good story will
keep them awake, and quicken their breathing, till
you can reach their minds with a good idea and fool
them into swallowing a great truth.

Why should I care whether they are amused or not?
I refuse to play buffoon to any one! I assert that all
writers of novels and stories and plays have been buffoons, paid to tickle the imaginations of men, as fid-
dlers tickle their ears and women the rest of them.

Most men are children, even at sixty, and they need
these time-killers; they need fiction and adventure;
they need the picturesque and the pathetic. Authors,
even though not quite children themselves, have been
ready to fill the bill, getting down on all fours on the
floor, blowing a tin horn, and straddling a broom-stick.

I am sorry to say that among them have been men I admire considerably: Homer and Cervantes, Shakespeare and Dostoievski. They, like other buffoons, have asked: "What can I do for you to-day?" When I read them myself and enjoy them, I too am a captious child always eager to hear a story from mama!

I realize that I am hard to please—a bore and a Puritan. These men have brightened our childhood. Their people have walked with us and talked to us on many an evening of sadness and lust in our boyhood years. Who would have believed that they were just buffoons? Even I, when not obsessed with wrath that makes me vomit upon them, doubt my own words and almost believe I must be out of my mind, unjust, unkind.

But no, I am right. What is a clown? A clown is a man who amuses men. And how does he amuse them? Often by making them laugh at the misery of others; but at any rate, by using their unhappiness and their misfortunes as a means of arousing not compassion and horror, but mere curiosity. The sad case of two lovers who die before marrying is sure to keep off ten yawns an hour. The desperation of a mother, the infidelity of a wife, the vengefulness of a murderer, the despondency of a failure, the generosity of a martyr, the disaster of an innocent—is there anything in the world that is not seized upon by the professional story-teller and made his own, to be exposed at one-fifty a peep to the eyes of boys and girls who have more vital energy than they can find opportunity to use, and to papas and mamas who would enjoy a laugh at Don Quixote's expense and a tear or two over poor King Lear?

The object of all their art—and sometimes it is a great art—is to interest indolent readers or spectators, transport them outside their petty, narrow, personal lives, unenlightened, trivial, humiliating, burdensome. Give the word buffoon its highest, noblest, most heroic meaning, if you will! But let me apply it to those who seek some recompense for amusing by writing, though their reward be a dead branch of laurel, an epigraph on a tombstone, a round of applause in a theater, or ten thousand dollars cash.

Do you think such things befit men conscious of their place in this mysterious and awe-inspiring universe? Do you think that the few of us who can see four spans farther than these children and know the end awaiting us if we do not courageously conquer destiny—upbuilding a purer life against the menace of ultimate Nothingness—do you think, I ask, that we should encourage such childishness and fatuity in men, stopping them in front of cardboard theaters to watch the antics of dreamland puppets, and listen to the joys and woes of silly phantoms?

Why all this misplaced compassion? Why waste so much genius in amusing and soothing men? How much finer, how much more dangerous it would be to startle them from their slumbers, bring them face to face with the darkness about us, dangle them head down into the Abyss of Nothing, forcing them to rouse themselves, know themselves, become sadder but nobler in the face of a universe which now barely concedes them life!

Away with novels, stories, legends, tragedies! If you're bored, there's bridge! Or try a bath in the salt sea! Let genius no longer be used to furnish entertainment for idlers, to reanimate people who have once been or will never be—but rather to proclaim new, and better lives, to prepare an earth that will know no sorrow save the sorrows of the spirit, and bring forth men bent not on forgetting, but on remembering and promising!

Chapter 41: Certainty

I DO not ask for bread, for fame, for pity.

I do not ask women for kisses, bankers for money, "geniuses" for praise. These things I can do without, or I can steal them, or earn them. What I ask for and plead for humbly, on bended knee, with all the fervor and all the passion of my soul is: a little certainty. Something I can believe in with surety, just one, small, tiny atom of unquestionable Truth!

In the name of all you hold most precious, by your life, by your latest love, by your favorite dream—tell me, is there one among you who has what I seek? Is there one among you who is *certain,* who is *sure*— who *knows* that he lives and moves in *Truth?* If there be one such, and if he prove to be not mistaken or misled (and as generous as he is fortunate!), let him tell me *what* he knows! Let him tell me what his *Truth* is! I will hear it under oath of secrecy! I will pay him any price he asks. I will pay him when and where he pleases.

I must have a little certainty—I need something that is true. I cannot do without it. I cannot live unless I have it. I ask for nothing else. I ask for nothing more. A large order, a most unusual request— that I know! But I must make this request at any cost—I must have it granted in any possible way. If my life matters to any one in this world, let him give me what I seek, no matter what the charge!

I have never sought anything else. From my earliest days I have lived for nothing else. I have knocked at all doors, I have scanned all eyes, I have watched all lips, I have fathomed a thousand, yes, ten thousand hearts. In vain! In vain have I thrown myself into life, even to the point of drowning and nausea; and in vain, ever in vain, have I ruined my eyes reading the old and the latest books. In vain have I deafened my brain with the wranglings of numberless rival philosophers. In vain, eternally in vain, have I turned inward upon myself, harkening to inner voices, humbly preparing the way for the great revelation. But nothing! Absolutely nothing came, and no one answered me!

No one, at least, has given me an answer that satisfied my longing, relieved me of further need of asking. Nothing has calmed my all too impatient hunger, or slaked my all too burning thirst. Not all these efforts of mine, not all my trials and struggles were wholly wasted: many obstructions fell, many walls were torn down and leveled—some gently crumbling like caving sand, others with a thunderous roar, as if a new earth were bursting from the old earth. But behind every partition, emptiness; beyond every wall, darkness; and an echo so perverse that to every "yea" of hope there answered a faint but never-ending "nay"!

It can never be said that I lacked courage. I remember long clear nights that I spent, awake, out of doors—the illusion of the Infinite in my soul—over my head such skies and such stars as give health to the body and cleanse the mind of the bestial colors of day. . . . Then I looked into the microscope—and what did I see? Just what I see daily with my naked eyes—tiny creatures in a tiny world—devouring one another!

There came men of faith and men sworn to preserve the Faith. But though they reasoned with me they could not give me the faith that was in their words. For where there were words there were no deeds; and in their words my accurst intelligence discerned deceit, and pride, and illusion, and ignorance, and sham, and interest, and calculation—all that would make of God the servant of man.

Nor did I have better luck with the philosophers. The best of them were grammarians who sharpened and sharpened their sickles till the grass was standing dead and dry in the fields and they were not yet ready to begin the harvest. And the rest were poets who had missed their calling, fanatics without charm who spent days and nights over plans of celestial utopias where no one could live, building tall and costly palaces with imposing fronts, but no walls or rooms behind.

And no truth anywhere! No truth, I mean, of the kind that strikes one prostrate to earth like a flash of divine lightning from on high, and illumines everything, inside and out with unextinguishable brilliancy —man and his image!

No certainty anywhere! Everything its pro and its con—each con its pro, and each pro its con! Ideas, I could see, were all diamonds and prisms, four-faced godheads, sphinxes with a thousand answers to every ten questions. Never can we say of a thing: "It is thus and so and not otherwise." No problem can be answered in one way, and in that way only. Every man who speaks has a right on his side and the man who contradicts him has his right also, and so with the man who contradicts both the first and the second; and so with a possible fourth. With each in his turn we have to agree. Even the lunatic has his "case" and we must hear it patiently.

A skeptic, I? No—alas! Not even a skeptic. The skeptic is in luck. He at least has one faith left— faith that certainty is impossible.

A skeptic can be at his ease and, if he likes, dogmatic. But not I! I do not even believe in the uselessness of research. I am not even sure that certainty is non-existent. There is always a chance that truth may be found. There is always the chance that some one may have it.

Why not I? What does it mean that I have not found it, that I am not the one who has it? Now, at any rate, I refuse to go on living thus. I refuse to be torn as I now am torn between doubt and negation. I refuse to be tormented by this endless yearning, crushed by this ever-recurring defeat. I want some one to help me, I want him who has found his peace to share a little of his peace with me.

But not words, understand! Not tricks! No fairy stories! No "fond hopes"! No female chatter!

I must have a certainty that is certain—just one; a belief that cannot be shaken—just one; a truth that is true, be it ever so small—just one!

A truth that will let me touch the innermost substance of the world—the last and most solid prop of reality, a truth that so firmly lays hold on the mind that to conceive its opposite is impossible; a truth that is *knowledge,* perfect, definite, authentic, undebatable *knowledge.*

Without this truth I cannot live. If no one has pity on me, if no one can answer me, in death will I seek the blessedness of True Light, or the peace of Eternal Nothingness.

Chapter 42: Let Misfortune Come!

THERE come moments when I *feel well,* when I seem happy, when I have the cowardly courage to forget the degradation and torture of my life. And at such times, slyly, slowly, softly,—lest conscience hear!—I let myself down into the comforts and consolations and indulgences of your fat, lazy, peaceful, meaningless lives, O detestable, contemptible comrades mine!

A shameful thing to confess! But I confess it, shuddering!

I am not made for joy! I must not seek comforts. Woe unto me if I let myself fall into the warm and languorous embrace of pleasure! To be true to the principle of my soul's being, to the vows I made when I was born again, to the pact I signed with life and death, I cannot dissolve, I cannot be soaked up, in the milky pap of common everyday comfort.

In my life there is too much regularity, too much peace, too much comfort already. While the Son of Man has no place to lay His head, I have a flat with five rooms in an old palace. Near it is a park of beauties that are ever new. The sun shines in at my windows. I have comfortable beds to sleep in, luxurious chairs to sit in, deep plates to eat from. I am poor, yet I have an abundance. Every day a thick soup steams on my table, and a crisp white bread crunches under my teeth. The world has at last a faint smile for the youth who once chose to flee from it like a disinherited son!

Nowadays every phase of my life is well ordered, smooth running. I go to bed early and sleep until morning. My stomach is in top form. I have friends who are fond of me. Women come my way. The great and the small lift their hats when I go by. All is well and I lack nothing. All is well, I lack nothing —in the eyes of the man who looks only at the outside, and judges by his own measure.

But it was not for this that I came into the world. It was not for this that I consented to live. It was not for this that over twenty long years I have been torturing, flagellating my spirit as the mad monks of old tortured and lashed their breasts and shoulders. I have stayed in the world because the world is more fearful than Nothingness. I accepted life because life is more painful than death. I have stabbed, flayed, hammered myself, because agony alone begets truth, because the offspring of the mind is not born without anguish. All music is but sadness. And the bottom of the Bitter Cup is the only joy which brings not loathing.

I have no desire to be content, peaceful, happy, rich. I call all misfortunes down on my head! I invoke disasters without end upon the pathway of my life! May fevers make my teeth chatter! May poverty empty my house! May love betray me! May my friends desert me! May vermin slaver my flesh!

May delirium and madness rule my brain! May enemies persecute and assail me! May all my dear ones die at my side, stricken with sudden death! May all the sorrows of the world be mine!

But on this one condition: that it be proven whether I am a man or a good-for-nothing, whether I am held upright by a mind or only by a backbone. My hair turns gray. My cheeks grow flabby. My forehead wrinkles. My eyes run with tears. But what does it matter? The flowers I seek grow only in hopeless solitude—flowers that never fade, and never droop their heads, flowers enduring forever in eternal fragrance!

Chapter 43: The Disintegration of the Body

NOT only is my mind failing. My body too is going to the bad.

Too long have I gone about crying: Spirit, Spirit! I have given no thought to my body. I have kept it in check with spur and bit, like a restive stallion. I hoped to break it in. I counted on mastering it, gripping it by its mind, taming it without even looking it once in the eye. Now it is taking its revenge. I feel that the end is drawing near. This frame work of lanky bones with a scanty wrapping of flesh shows signs of collapsing—dust unto dust, dust under dust.

Especially my eyes. I hurt them while I was still a boy, on long nights of reading by candle light, or under the steadier but fainter glow of a little oil lamp, which almost always burned lower and lower and finally went out at midnight, leaving me in the dark with the filthy smell of the wick still smoking from some smoldering filament. I hurt them on winter afternoons of lingering twilights (what a bore to stop in the middle of an interesting page and leave my warm chair to get a match!). I hurt them in the dark reading rooms of antiquated libraries—where I would read and read as long as I could guess at the shape of a letter or write and write as long as my pen could feel its way across the sheet of unruled paper. Often in the morning, when the first rays of dawn filtered through my shutters, I would pick up the book I had been forced to put down the night before, and read until sheer disgust for the animal warmth of my sheets would drive me out into the cold streets to my daily tasks.

Straining in the red murky lamplight of evenings and in the faint whiteness of dawns, the pupils of my eyes dilated beyond measure and the lids grew inflamed. My eyes ached all day long and spilled tears down my cheeks. I paid no attention then; but for some time past I have not been able to tell what is on top of a hill, nor recognize a well-known face a few steps away.

My eyes are not good. I can see only things that are close at hand and then only with the help of very strong glasses. The bright colors of the world, its finer and more delicate outlines, are lost for me. Everything is blurred as though draped in a mist—a mist which is light and transparent, for the present, but which is everywhere and never lifts. At night all distant figures lose their sharpness. I might mistake a man for a woman, a stationary lantern for a streak of red light, a boat coming down the river for a blotch of black on its current. People's faces are spots of white to me; windows in house fronts spots of black; trees are dark solid streamers rising from darkness. Only three or four of the brightest stars shine in the sky for me.

And, oh, that this much would last! But I am afraid I shall go blind. I am afraid that I shall see less and less; and in the end—nothing! It terrifies me to think what my life will be then. I have no resources outside my mind. My best friends are among the Dead. I have no pleasure outside of books. And—unable to read! Never again to see any of those beautiful letters, round, italic, or Elzevirian, that have given me such great joys, taught me all I know, expressed for others all that is best in me. Dependent upon the kindness of people, reading through eyes of strangers, at the mercy of the preference, the patience, the compassion of others! Around me, darkness—total darkness! Blackness, obscurity everywhere—for ever! I, *alone* with my thoughts, *alone* in the dark—until death!

I never really believe this; yet I think of it from time to time as though it were a certainty, fixed in advance, a question of days or of years. I try to live, in my imagination, the wretched life I foresee. Sometimes, when a street is deserted before me, I shut my eyes and walk ahead. I hesitate. I veer from side to side. I touch the plastered walls and the ornaments of the houses. I study the echo of my footsteps on the pavements. Could I get home, if I tried? Then I hear a noise: a carriage, some one coming! I open my eyes again. The world is not lost. I can still see! I am saved! I close my eyes again. Around me darkness, within me joy! And so I go on till I reach my destination.

But it is useless. I shall certainly go blind some day—I am sure of that! Already space is punctured before me at several points. Little black spots dance and whirl in front of my eyes and no lens dispels them. When they grow larger and finally unite, a black curtain of blindness will fall—never to rise again —between me and the wonderful world of sunshine and color. All will be over!

If I do not die blind I shall die a paralytic. My nerves too are spoiled and my brain is sick. For some time I have been noticing the warnings: aches and numbness in a leg; involuntary twitchings in my fingers; sharp stabbing pains in my head. Every now and then I feel a sensation of melting in my skull. When I try to think my mind gets muddled and clouded. Ideas vanish all of a sudden and I am unable to recall them; while some stupid word, some insignificant image, pops up in their place and stays there, refusing to be pushed back into the night of unconsciousness where it belongs. The air weighs heavy upon me as if I were supporting the world on my head, and inside all is emptiness and pain. I cannot work. I cannot think. I refuse to know anything. Tremendous apathy, fatigue, idleness—spiritual loss of appetite, from having drunk everything and vomited everything! Hatred of all ideas and all faces! I am an object of contempt and compassion in my own eyes.

More than once I have fainted at home or on the street; and then—long days of convalescence, of enforced rest, of indescribable humiliation, of impotent rage, of spasmodic purposeless strain. And nothing helps, nothing is able to galvanize me—neither coffee, nor tea, nor wine, nor women, nor good conversation. I am full of disgust. I am drowned in Nothingness. My one desire is for night-time and bed, for deep, dull bestial slumber that will last till high noon.

Aberrations now and then—caprices, strange whims, fixed ideas; and frightful in the midst of it all, that terrifying confusion, that oppression, that heaviness of head which is not only headache but soul ache—anemia of the mind, dumb shame at a hated but necessary rest! There are moments when I seem unable to grasp a thought again. Distorted fancies, impossible figures, disjointed fragments and phrases race in a mad shrieking dance through my brain. I am caught up in the whirl, lost in the tumult of my own creations. Lights vault over each other, appear and disappear in a black sea. Then the haggard fainting weariness of one who does not belong to a world no longer his and who eats only because he would get close again to a bodily health that is solid and tangible!

One of these days the crisis will not pass. One side of my body will fall motionless, forever. My brain will not act, will not think, will not see what it saw, nor remember what it has seen, will not understand the thoughts of others, nor correlate and express its own. A sluggish stirring of a few idiotic, meaningless, unrelated images! White, all around: whitewashed walls, white aprons, a white sky above that holds no secrets, the hustling tranquillity of a respectable, a private, sanatorium!

Or perhaps—wild shrieks, monstrous fears, terrifying nights of phantoms and lamentations in the darkness of a mind and the darkness of a padded room!

Or perhaps—a slow unconscious fading away—never understanding again, never comprehending again, never knowing again, ever, ever—not even understanding that there is no understanding! And—the end . . .

Wherein I have sinned shall I be punished! I have read so many useless things, I have thought so many stupid and disgusting thoughts! So—never shall I read again! Never shall I think again! Shadows without, emptiness within . . .

Finis!

"We shall stand with heads high as long as the day lasts; and what we can do ourselves we shall not leave to be done by those who come after us."

GOETHE.

Chapter 44: Death

BUT who said I was going to die?

Die? Shall I too some day suddenly stop breathing, seeing, moving, suffering? Must I do as others do— as all do?

All men die!

Thank you! But is that any reason why I should die too? Dying is all right for those who like that form of amusement. I am Myself—not some one else!

Come now, let's talk sense! There must be some mistake here, a big mistake. What earthly reason can there be that I too should disappear, stupidly, like the first nobody who comes along! Don't you know who I am? I carry the whole world inside me! Don't you know? If I die there will be no rain to fall and spatter on the leaves; no beautiful warm sun to give you a tan; no green-white fields of alfalfa to become billowing seas of shadow as the wind caresses them; no vast blue sky; no calm white oxen; no Madonnas on shields of gold in the depths of dark churches; no frenzied songs from the lips of jilted maidens; no jewels to sparkle at night in show-windows in the red glare of electric lights!

The whole world with its beauties and its horrors, with its ideas and its material forms—the whole world is here, in me, within my very Self! And if I were to die it would be—cancelled.

So you say I must die like anybody else—turn into a clammy corpse, into stinking carrion, a mess of squirmy worms, a handful of dust, a fistful of muck!

How could I possibly think such a thing of myself? This world will suddenly die with me? All I carry in my heart and brain—this ceaseless stirring of thoughts, memories, fancies, struggles,—all over, over for ever? How can that be? Is that just? How can I imagine the world going on if I can think it only in *my* thoughts?

Off with you, malicious and insidious deceivers, hyenas hungering for carcasses! I cannot die! I have no intention of dying! And I won't die!

I suppose you think that I am hanging on to life because I am happy, beatified, contented—lolling in comforts, rolling in money?

Far from it! I am the world's most unhappy and miserable man. I have no loves, no riches, no friends. I am not handsome. I am not strong. The world has given me but few joys. I have rarely tasted pleasure. I have often wept. I have almost always suffered. And yet—I do not want to die. I refuse! I refuse! I intend to go on living. I insist on living forever.

My dear parson: don't come and bore me with talk about other worlds—a calmer, more beautiful, more luminous life. I don't believe it. I know nothing about any such worlds. I will have none of the happiness you promise. This is the world I know, this earth, this hideous, gloomy, tumultuous life. This is the life I want. This is the life I must have. This is the life

I ask for—forever. Yes, this miserable, wretched, unhappy, disgusting life with all its misery and wretchedness and unhappiness and sorrow. A glimpse of sky through a half-opened window! The song of a bird on a morning of springtime! The laugh of a baby and of a woman. A word I can write to some one who loves me. The quivering shadow of a tree on a wall, shining white under an August moon!

Chapter 45: But for That Very Reason

IT would be difficult, I believe, to find a man who has made a greater failure of his life. I have nothing left to lose. All the strings and props which keep others on their feet have been cut in my case—those which are dropped from heaven (faiths and beliefs), as well as those which attach to the earth (dogmas and principles). I am a bottom to the Pit of Evil. I have denied my God. I had to deny Him; I deserted my faith and the faithful abandoned me.

Knowledge does not suffice me. Men disgust me—women even worse! Literature turns my stomach; inspiration fails; fame nauseates. My life is dirty and irksome; my body is rotting. My one first supreme and innermost desire—Power—is now not even a desire. All my tables of value were broken in the course of my inner convulsions. All hope has paled in the darkness of these years. The anchors that might have saved me have proved to be hooks, fastening me to earth, to a life that has no promise, no allurement. The performance is over; the scenery has been turned to the wall; the lights are out. The singers have shed their royal gowns and driven off in taxis in their plain black dresses. There lie the violins, abandoned, voiceless, beside scores that will never be opened again. The last fête has ended with the last note, which still vibrates across a dark stage sounding the key of this all too empty silence.

But two roads are now left open: total imbecility or suicide.

And yet I still feel an immense will to live. I refuse to die. I want to start over again, do my life over again—find other reasons for living—living, if need be, suspended in the void, with no strings above my head, no props behind my back, no crutches under my arms; but living, living! Living in the full sense of the word; living with eye and hand, with brain and liver—living ten, twenty, thirty years, until I have learned to make my voice heard in the discordant choruses of men.

I refuse to die either halfway or altogether—either in mind or in body. I have in me something stronger than all defeat—a rock set up in the full tide of my soul, unshaken of the breakers that have crashed over it. In me is a beast with an appetite, with two legs that must walk, with a head that must think, with a hand that must write. But why? In the name of what faith? With what goal in view? The beast knoweth not. The beast has no intelligence; the beast has no religion—the beast is just a beast: it will not down! Though the banners have been lowered the ramparts still stand. If words fail to fit the facts, to hell with words and long live the facts! Fact resists and exists. Fact is irrefutable and tyrannical. Fact will not down!

It is not only my blood that refuses to think of ceasing. My very Self refuses to abdicate—my Self, which closed one by one the windows opening on "the Possible," and was driven even from the one window which still held it, the window on "the Impossible." And there it stands in the darkness with no appetites and no powers. But it refuses to down! It waits. It hopes for nothing, but—it waits. If the worst comes it will accept it, but it will not lie down there where Nothing begins—Nothing without even the hope of sorrow!

My deeper Self has been crushed and tortured in its every fiber; yet it rejoices in its torment, for that torment means life, that torment means struggle. That Destiny persecutes it in such fashion is proof to the Ego of its worth as a victim, gives it a sense of its importance in the universe. Down and down it has gone to the depths of the abyss. It can go no further. Either it must there dig its grave or go back upward again toward the light. There is no other choice.

So the man who has failed rises again and begins a new chapter.

But this new chapter is in no way like the others. The things I denied stand denied. Abandoned dreams will not be dreamed again. I repell to-day the ambitions I despised yesterday. The men I loathed I still hold at arm's length. The goals which at one time dazzled my eyes are still far away.

But what does that matter? A new road lies before me—the secret is revealed. A last possibility of greatness is looming in my path and I do not reject it.

Because of it, because of it alone, flowers are again blooming in the desert of my mind, and the pupils of my eyes, shrinking in shame behind their red lids, sparkle and flash once more. I can still be a hero! Against self-destruction I set up self-esteem. It is this—this *nothing*, that saves me.

For me there is nothing left. I am an out-and-out nihilist. I no longer believe in anything. I am an out-and-out skeptic. I no longer believe in anything. I am the perfect, the accomplished, the definitive atheist. An atheist who does not kneel even to the secular, the rational, the philosophical, the humanitarian beliefs that have replaced the ancient mythologies. I know that our efforts all come to nothing. I know the end of us all is nothing. I know that at the end of Time, the reward of our toil will be nothing— and again nothing. I know that all our handiwork will be destroyed. I know that not even ash will be left from the fires that consume us. I know that our ideals, even those we achieve, will vanish in the eternal darkness of oblivion and final non-being. There is *no* hope, none, in my heart. *No* promise, none, can I make to myself and to others. No recompense can I expect for my labors. No fruit will be born of my thoughts. The Future—eternal seducer of all men, eternal cause of all effects—offers me nothing but the blank prospect of annihilation.

Yet, face to face with this terrible outlook, face to face with this dread despair, caught as I am in a race toward Nothing, I do not wince, I do not draw back. I am still willing to live on. All my doing will be *useless,* but for *that very reason* I am compelled to *do*. Nothing—the Nothingness of myself, of my work, of the world entire—is the final goal of all my efforts. And yet *for that very reason* I will go on striving till the earth enfolds me in its black embrace.

I repudiate all my utilitarian past. Men want something for all they do. Even such actions as seem prompted of the spirit—acts of love, faith, creation— expect an equivalent return, ask, sooner or later, for payment. Nothing for nothing! Even religions, the arts, the philosophies, all are based on gain. Every human act without exception is a note of exchange which demands cash. The date of maturity varies. Some notes fall due in another life, in heaven, or in ages to come—but the day of reckoning will fall at last. If men were convinced that any part of their labor would be unrecompensed forever they would stop work right where they are. Even God insists upon His reward in prayers and sacrifices. He has reserved a special section in Hell's prison for His bad risks.

In times past, I have been the most greedy of all graspers. I wanted everything in return for a little. For a few years of solitude, of study, of climbing, I asked eternal omnipotence. I wanted the Spirit not for the Spirit's sake, but as a lever to pry things, an instrument to all worldly possessions.

Now that that has all crumbled before my eyes, now that I know nothing save that the Infinite is unsolvable and that all labor is futile, now I strangle the seeker, the utilitarian, the robber, the extortioner, the cut-throat, that is within me. I consent to live for the very reason that there is no wage for living, and I continue to think precisely because thought can never draw its salary.

The desperate man finds on the rock-bottom of his despair a foothold for a rebound that will take him far above the hell-pits where the mere whimperers whimper. In the tragic vacuity of his soul, the atheist —who believes in no gods, in no man, in no thing— finds the strength to believe in *himself*, in the present moment of his being, in the world of which he is a part. After the orgy of anguish is over the possibility of joy springs triumphant from the very bosom of torment. Since I hope for nothing I cannot be disappointed; I shall not be downcast at the spineless failures of *fact*.

The man who is alone, who stands on his own feet, who is stripped bare, who asks for nothing and wants nothing, who has reached the apex of disinterestedness not through blind renunciation but through excess of clear vision, turns to the world which stretches out before him as a burned prairie, as a devastated city —a world in which no churches, asylums, refuges, ideals, are left—and says: "Though you promise me nothing I am still with you, I am still an atom of your energies, my work is part of your work; I am your companion and your mirror as you march on your merciless way."

So long as a man expects something from this universe, he is only a trader out for what he can get, exchanging, bargaining. He is angry if he fails; he kills himself if he cannot meet his obligations, if his notes are not paid, if receipts do not cover disbursements. But the man who has renounced every recompense in advance and does work which will be undone, *knowing* that it will be undone, is the only man worthy, really worthy, of living happily in this universe. In a world of shopkeepers, he alone is a *noble,* though the signboards the traders have hung on their shops boast of the excellence, purity, and genuineness of their wares.

He does his work without expecting any one to do it for him; he gives knowing that he never will receive; he strives for the heights knowing he will never attain them; he gives his whole Self knowing he will never be justly rewarded. But in this precisely lies his tragic grandeur—in this lies his detachment from humanity which still binds him to men. Other joys are denied him. Unlike those who believe in life, in humanity, in truth, he has no promised consolations, no self-deceptions, no illusions to help him along on his way and make his road easier. He has no strength but his own to rely on; and his knowledge that he is strong enough to do without all the rest, fills his soul with a wholesome, though bitter, joy. What courage, what virtue, is there in living when we are sure our hopes will become realities; that some sort of paradise, earthly or celestial, is waiting to comfort us for all our troubles? Man's real nobility and his greatest heroism lie in his being able to go on living, when he knows there is no reason for his living; when all the poultices and crutches that make life endurable have been cast aside.

To achieve this nobility, this greatness, this last and desperate heroism, I shrink both from death and from mediocrity. I go on living, I insist on living, and I *shall* live without fear of disillusionment and of defeat.

I have been a total failure. But from that failure springs my strength for a new victory.

Chapter 46: The Return to Earth

So then, I am alive again. But *alone,* terribly *alone.* Just myself—not a god, not God; but, like Him, uninterested in the whole business, since I could not be master of things like Him!

I must reconstruct my life along new lines—a life all my own, a real life, a new life. Just myself—no allies, no companions! No helping hand to steady me should I stumble on the upward path. The world is full of voices: but it is a case of "glad tidings of great joy"; and of such I have had a bellyful. Your "glad tidings" are for other ears, for people who have not been freed. To me they are empty words.

Yet in making myself over, in straightening my course, in starting on a new journey I need something to lean on; I must take root again somewhere. I have only myself; but that Self is more tightly bound to one part of the universe than to other parts. I am not just a metaphysical absolute floating in an atmosphere of concept. I was born in a certain spot; I belong to a certain race, I have behind me a certain tradition and a certain history. To concentrate, to collect myself, means simply closer contact with my native soil, with my people, with the culture from which, willy-nilly, I have come.

I must start from the beginning again. I must be

born again, reënter the womb again,—not a womb of
flesh, my mother's, but a truer and greater one: my
native land. As long as I was but a thinking maniac,
the world was my country and my nation was the
bookshop where I found the only laws I was bound to
respect. But now that I intend to recast my bones,
to start a new blood flowing in my veins, I must return to the deepest roots of my concrete being.

So I determined to become acquainted with my
birthplace all over again, and my rediscovery of my
old home was the rediscovery of my own soul. Doc-
tors often prescribe for their patients the atmosphere
of their native regions. Happily, I, the convalescent
in this case, was much improved by a breath of my
native air. So long as I was buried in theory and in
universals I remained a man of the city, of houses. I
forgot the country, or if I ever went back to it, I did
not see it; I did not open my arms to it; I did not
love it. But our Mother's face can be seen only from
the high lands, far from the painting and powdering
of the towns. Up here on the mountain tops I have
found her again—reddened in the sunlight, pale under
the moon, white with the snow, freshened with flowers,
wrinkled by the wind, never old, ever young, ever the
same, with a smile that is not a smile of dissimulation.

In vain may I try to twist my suffering self into an
Athenian god, or a Scandinavian athlete. As a brain,
as a brain merely, I can talk with a Chinaman and
with a Sufi, with a German professor and an English
essayist, with a French Jacobin and a Greek sophist.

I belong to all ages and all races. I understand. I am understood. My words are in international coinage. I can spend them in any market. But the moment I crawl into my shell, mind and body, brain and heart, the moment I would really get inside a race, or inside an era of history, it is to this age that I belong, it is to this spot that I am rooted. No matter what I do I am a Tuscan, born among Tuscans, on Tuscan soil, among Tuscan values—born in Tuscany in 1881, twenty years old in the first year of this century, and writing now this year of our Lord one thousand nine hundred and twelve. I am not only an Italian, but a Tuscan. A man's true country is not the kingdom, or republic, where he is born. Italy is too big for the individual Italian. Our genuine countries must be small. Even in France, a nation closely knit if any ever was, the man from Brittany feels himself a stranger to the man from Provence; and the Norman or the Alsatian is Norman or Alsatian even in the heart of Paris.

I feel that I am very deeply a Tuscan. To me Neapolitans and Venetians are foreigners; I feel they are further removed from me than some barbarians. I am not happy in their company. We are not brothers. The fact that men write the same language and are governed by the same laws does not make them countrymen.

Even among Tuscans I often feel aloof, a stranger. When I say Tuscany I mean particularly a rural Tuscany, the mountains, the hills, the rivers, the horizons that stretch from the rosy turrets of the Apuans to the vast lonely marshes of the Maremma, from the towering peaks of the Apennines to the heaving green of the Tuscan sea. I mean these skies that are beautiful even when they are ugly, the silvery pallor of our gnarled olive trees, our cypresses straight and erect as lances, the heavy grapevines festooned across our hillsides, our desolate rocky valleys where only the purple thistle and the sulphur broom can force their way up between the stones.

And when I say Tuscany, I mean the great Tuscans and their genius: I mean the Etruscan fathers keeping their slumbering vigils in their tombs, as calm and as shrewd as seers—the Etruscans who came from the Orient bringing the love of the future and the certain promise of art; the Etruscans who taught civilization to the Romans, and drew their boundaries about that part of Italy which was to foster her greatest sons; and so on down to the impetuous Dante, the dry and tart Macchiavelli, the overpowering Michelangelo, the insatiate Leonardo, the deep-seeing Galileo. In all these men one feels muscle, fiber, strength, a current of vulgar forceful realism, sobriety, clarity, greatness without inflation and rhetoric, without bigotry and superstition. Tuscany has bred a genius all its own, which stands apart from every other type of genius, whether Italian or foreign. With this genius I feel myself in complete accord.

Finding myself meant, therefore, finding Tuscany, its soil and its tradition—a Tuscany that no longer

meant the roads about Florence running along between
gray walls and the villa gates of the wealthy, but trails
of goat-herds up over the backs of the Apennines—
alone with the skies above my head, alone with the
woods at my feet. No longer the urban heights of the
Vial dei Colli and the *Incontro;* but the humpbacked
summits of Pratomagno and the peaks of the Luna
Alps. All for myself I chose a hillock, hidden, remote,
unknown, that lies in the heart and at the same time
on the outskirts of my Tuscany. Near by are the
source of the Tiber, the wood where Saint Francis suffered, the castle where Michelangelo was born, the
village where Pier della Francesca first saw the light.
To a house not far from mine Carducci came as a boy
and a republican. From the hilltops above I can see
the Romagna seashore and the highlands of Umbria.

On this rocky hillside where the wind is never still,
my soul again found peace and itself. Within this
circle of glowering and jagged mountains, in this clearing, barren of flowers and grass but fertile with stones;
in the shadow of these hard and untrimmed oak trees;
within hearing of this narrow but clear-flowing stream
(dirty and overgrown when it reaches Rome!); under
this intensely blue sky (so delicate, so transparent,
even when scattered with clouds), I again inhaled the
fresh smell of the earth, drank in pure air, tasted real
bread, felt the honest warmth of burning cord-wood.
Step by step Life won me back with the beauty of its
simplicity. I became a child again and a primitive,
a savage, and a bumpkin. I united the bond that tied

me to my ancestors—plain peasants of the peasantry and good plebeian country folk, who herded cows and harvested corn in all this neighborhood. I made my peace with the old family. For this prodigal son, who had rioted at all the intellectual banquets of Europe and laid a whip to other people's swine, the old house found a welcome corner by its smoke-blackened fireplace, and a seat at the pine-board table creaking under yellow polenta, and salted hams and loaves of hot bread fresh from the oven.

During the first days, the joy of my discovery was so great that I had to take to my room actual pieces of this fraternal, paternal country, which I recognized and loved each day; sometimes a stone, pointed like a mountain, sometimes a gall apple loosened from the leaf of an oak, then, a smooth, well-modeled acorn or a bunch of wild flowers, or a cypress berry, or an ear of corn. All such simple, humble, unimportant, useless, common things gave me untold comfort: they were my friends, my family, parts of me, symbols of the earth from which I sprang, and of its tradition.

At the same time I turned to the writings of countrymen of mine who had gone before me. Since my first hungry years of omnivorous reading, I had rarely gone back to them. I had steeped myself in exotic things, scarcely reading an Italian book, and among Italians always preferring the thinkers to the poets, learning to imagination. When, up there, returning to my country of the present, I felt an unconquerable longing to go back to my country of the past. In the

shades of the beeches and the live-oaks, breathing in
the cool fragrance of spearmint, fanned by breezes
from the Vernia, I re-read, one by one, books which
were mine by right of birth and rebirth: Dante, Com-
pagni, Boccaccio, Sacchetti, Macchiavelli, Redi, Gino
Capponi, Giosuè Carducci. Books which I had read
out of curiosity or a sense of duty, which had bored
me at school and had failed to move me out of school,
which I had looked upon as lessons in rhetoric or as
historical monuments, now opened their pages to me
as friends and brothers, took on a new color, a richer
flavor, coming to life again in all their primitive vigor.
This "old stuff" made my spirit young again. These
substantial, unspoiled men of bygone days seemed to
me, in certain respects, more modern than I was. I
felt I belonged to their household, that I was one of
their family, that I spoke their language, that my
experiences enabled me to understand even things
which to strangers must seem vulgar and queer.

It was like the return of an exile to the places where
he was reared. I saw everything as if for the first
time. My mind was flooded with things that seemed
new to me, yet each in the place where it ought to be,
each in its appropriate frame. The potholes of Hell;
the beaming rivers of Paradise; Florence bristling with
towers and lances; incorrigible youths—rapers of vir-
gins, terrors of husbands; doddling old men now clowns
now rascals; princes sly and cruel; the natural unsophisticated wickedness of man; movements of stars
in the Infinite, and of wine in the wine vats; a history

of failures and of hopes; the Valdarno and the Maremma; the Casentino and the Mugello—all the fair land of Tuscany, with its men and its gardens, its skies and its fountains, from the tumults of the Commune to the backbitings of '59! My country crept back into my heart, snuggled warm against my warm flesh, opening its arms to me as a mother to a long-expected son who finally returns.

Not only was I captivated by the meaty substance of those books, but quite as much by the magnificent art with which they were made, by the marvelous language in which they were written. No ornament, no exaggeration, no lace work, no weakness, no bad taste —strong stuff simply done, all design, all relief, bronze and stone, not whipped cream or honey. Deep decisive lines, rough at times perhaps, but strong and clear, and never one too many. A language rich and ever new, full of short-cuts and expressive detours, but no padding, no softening, familiar, racy, popular, yet with no damage to solemnity and majesty. In these books, as in the mountains of my country, an apparent poverty, a wholesome simplicity, a stern joy—grandeur and freedom!

Tuscany, retouched in this way, is *my* Tuscany, but it is also the real and the glorious Tuscany—not the Tuscany of bastard Florentines, of aristocratic cabbage patches, of those tiny, suave, sweet, castrated, would-be writers, who, from the Seventeenth Century on, have been stinking up their province and making it contemptible.

To this rediscovered and greater Tuscany I, for my part, shall remain true; for to make myself over again I had to start from the ground up—from the place and from the moment of my birth. I am like the soil from which I sprang, and would resemble it more closely still. I can no longer do without the inheritance of my fathers, and remain deaf to the voices of brothers I live too late to have known.

First the whole world was in me. Later I found myself alone and almost without life. To get my strength back again, I had to get a new hold on that bit of earth to which I was most closely placed and related. Now I have suckled again at my first Mother's breast. Once again I have listened to her voice. A new blood is spurting through my veins. My tongue is loosened. I am ready to resume my journey along the road to my true destiny.

Chapter 47: Who Am I?

BUT what is that destiny? What am I?

Now that I have only my recovered strength and my desperate exaltation, I cannot seek inspiration in extraneous motives, I cannot trust to phantoms outside my self. All the gods—sacred and profane, Asiatic and European—have hidden their faces from me. I have no God before me. I have based my cause on Nothing, as the ferocious *Unicum*. The universe falls into two parts: I—and the rest.

Now this inner kernel of my being must give life to everything, must animate and transmute all that surrounds me, to help me to endure it. In this last and decisive battle I must stand without allies. If death overtakes me and does not halt in my presence, I am but a good-for-nothing, fit only to flounder and finally to rot in the boundless vat of uselessness.

You, and I, therefore, O hateful Universe! The fight is between you and me! Here I am on my feet again, with some difficulty, sore from many falls, but still erect from the waist up; ready to challenge you, ready to spit into this puddle of slime where spineless Abels thrust the Cains who do not obey the unwritten laws of the species. Hard indeed is the life of an egoist without the protection of friendly walls, the shelter of calm bays, the clasp of warm and cordial hands. However, I want a cane not to lean on, but to strike with.

Who, then, am I?

What is this capital I have at my disposal, all mine, inherited from no one, stolen from no one, but earned penny by penny with the sweat of my soul in the factory of experience, and now my only treasure, the little power I have—my real self, in a word?

Many people, friends and enemies alike, have tried to define me, to describe me, to fix my limits and outlines. I have listened. I have said nothing. I have smiled. Having covered half my visibly possible life, after quite a few trials and a long quarantine of solitude, I think that I know myself better than others do.

I am not a man of action, and I am not a philosopher. I like history but I will never be a cabinet minister. Theories attract me, but I will never write a system. I am neither a money changer nor a saint. I want money for the freedom it brings, but I have not the courage to drop other things to get it. I envy the great ascetics, but I do not believe in gods or in heavens. In this jumble of health and disease, of philistinism and wickedness, which is of interest to me alone, there are but two aspects which can interest others.

I am, to say the whole thing in two words, a poet and an iconoclast, a dreamer and a skeptic, a lyrist and a cynic. How these two souls of mine can live and get along together it would take too long to tell. Yet such is the sum and substance of my individuality.

There are moments when I am just a pitiable senti-
mentalist, moved to tears as the mere tune of a Vien-
nese waltz, tortured on a piano, filters through my
drawn shutters on a quiet night; or again, a child
overflowing with tenderness as I gaze at an overcast
sky, stupidly gray, without even the cheer of a black
or white cloud; or again, an unfortunate wretch able
to tremble with love for an old man I do not know,
for a dead friend, for a broken flower, for a house with
doors and windows barred.

On the other hand there are times when I become the
wolf of Hobbes, with fangs that must needs tear and
bite. Nothing is sacred to me, not the greatness of
the great dead, nor glories tested by centuries, nor
truths proved by ages of experience, nor the sanctity
of laws, nor the majesty of codes, nor the axioms of
ethics, nor the ties of deepest affection. I am ready
to turn everything upside down, to destroy religions,
to expose the ugly side of every imposing front, the
blemishes on every star, the meanness and smallness
of every grandeur, the cowardliness underlying every
revered institution, the blindness of every sage, the infamy of every moralist, the right of every wrong, the
beauty of every evil, the infinitude of Nothing itself.
I revel in rending, stinging, offending, in lifting veils,
stripping corpses, tearing off masks. I am without
fear, without shame. I respect no man. I am happy
in a fight. I glory in confusing, in frightening, in seeming and in being cruel.

But this orgy of destruction over, the fanciful

dreamer comes to the fore in me, making up impossible stories, distorting realities, projecting his most evil instincts, his maddest longings upon the convenient mirror of his imagination, drawing caricatures of the men he hates and of the men he loves, taking a hint from life itself, then elongating and magnifying it in his dream to gigantic proportions.

At such times I am beset by absurd stories, crazy plans, unbelievable adventures, by madmen and criminals, who have never lived and are trying to come to life in me; by fictitious and unreasonable loves, by strange and horrible deaths. In the long periods when, like every one else, I am a bourgeois and a realist, I am forced to create a new world, in which I am the first to be unsettled and disturbed, a world which contains fragments and flashes of profound truth, but which is not the real living world we all think we know. Within the confines of this world I move with absolute freedom. I give the creatures of my fancy the faces I want them to have. I make them speak the language I like to hear. I have them live for purposes no living man would choose and then die suddenly by their own hands for reasons that would seem ridiculous to men of flesh and blood.

In any case, however, I remain the man who *refuses to accept the world*. This attitude is the common principle of unity and consistency in my two incoherent souls. Since I refuse to accept the world as it is, now I try to refashion it with my imagination, now I try to reform it by first breaking it to pieces. I re-

build with my art, I demolish with thought and logic
—two opposite processes which nevertheless converge
and harmonize.

Taken as I am, and as I shall always be—it is too
late to change!—I feel that I too am a force both of
creation and of dissolution, that I am a real value, and
have a right, a place, a mission, among men. Only
imbeciles condemned to imbecility for life can avow
satisfaction with this world. If a man tries to stir, to
animate, to inflame, to renew, to broaden it, he has
the right—not to gratitude, for which I do not give a
hang—but to freedom of speech and freedom of life.
To live at all every man must believe he is not altogether useless. I do not ask, do not desire, any
other support; but I too must have this pitiable assurance, quite as much as the weaklings. I live and act
knowing that my life and all I do will end in Nothing. But I demand that others admit my right to be
among them, and to offend them, for in so doing I am
doing something for their good.

In a world where people think only of eating and
making money, of amusing themselves and bossing
others, some one must, from time to time, throw a
new light on things, disclosing the extraordinary that
is in the ordinary, the mystery that is in the obvious,
the beauty that is in the dust pan. In a large and
powerful caste made up of slaves of opinion and tradition, of parasitic and sophistic pedants, of preachers
of old fairy stories, of jailers to moral and mystic jails,
of loquacious parrots prating of musty moral and social

norms and mildewed commonplaces, there should be, I say, an alarm clock, a night clerk, a sentry to stand guard over pure intellect, a brawny wielder of the pick-ax, an incendiary with a zest for arson, some one eager to burn up and to tear down—to clear the way for the light of the open spaces, for the trees of re-conquered liberty, for future experiments and achievements.

I am one of those men who undertake the most thankless tasks, who go where there is most danger. In return for the good and the evil I deliberately do, I claim the right to breathe, to warm myself at the fire, to walk, to lift my head, to spit in people's faces, to live according to my own law.

Chapter 48: My Style

I DO not write for money. I do not write to improve my complexion. I do not write to make my way with shy girls and fat men. Nor even do I write to twine the gay wreath of a reputation around my ragged slouch hat.

I write just to get the stuff off my mind—as a cesspool drains off its superfluous sewage. Yes, just that, you delicate, you proper people—proper as a baritone out for a walk!

Yes, to get the muck out of my mind! Notice: I do not say "to liberate my spirit" as does your long-haired hero and eponym, your philistine of philistines, Wolfgang von Goethe, intimate adviser of the Duke of Weimar, and of many rehabilitated stealers of fire.

He got his "liberation" through the tragic frivolities of a Werther—the tenuous despair of a voluntary exile; and the product of all this liberating made its way to the make-up tables of sentimental prostitutes, and to the bedsides of future suicides,—a deadly plaything, but wrapped in lace with all the frills and trimmings of well-bred literature.

I, on the other hand, get rid of the stuff inside me; and I think of the process in the most vulgar and nauseating terms. I mean the sputum that gathers in my catarrhed throat, and which spatters in every

sneeze I write on faces I would also like to punch.
I mean the bilious vomit that the spectacle of life
about me draws up into my stomach. I mean the pus
that oozes from the wounds and ulcers of my immoral
Self, exposed to contagion in this world, the most
crowded of pest houses. I mean the thunderous belch
that rises, like my contempt, from deep down in me!
No, my friends, I warn you, nothing ladylike will
ever come from my hurrying pen.

Rather than pale ink I would have on my pen-point
blood that is dark and streaming, like the gore that
flows from the breast of a hero stabbed in a midnight
brawl. I would have the metal tear and burn the
paper like a red-hot iron, that an acrid but head-clean-
ing smoke might rise from the scorched furrow to the
open nostrils of him who reads.

O respectable public mine, I never write with the
fussy humility of a butler handing you your hat and
coat. There are authors who stand toward their reader
like a counterfeit Neapolitan whining open-mouthed,
thrumming a guitar, under the windows of a winter
boarding-house—in hopes of a tip! Others, like long-
haired Magdalens, prostrate themselves at the reader's
feet, with vases of balms and ointments for all the
corns and raw spots on his soul. Others remind me of
the acolytes in starched collars who wave their censers
back and forth on Sundays between the screams of
the mass!

No, I belong to a different species. I was not born
to the calm regular breathing of the ox and the ass.

No meek shepherds whispered baby talk to me on the first day of my life. I was born a revolutionary; and I am not so sure that my first greeting to this world, rather than the regulation cry of surprise, was not a bar of music from some improper Marseillaise. No matter what the government of the world may be I shall always be against it! The natural attitude of my mind is one of protest. The instinctive posture of my body is one of attack. My favorite form of speech is invective and insult. Every love song turns on my lips into a refrain of revolt. My warmest effusions suddenly end in a titter of laughter, a sneer, an angry shrug of the shoulders. Oh, that my every word were a bullet whistling through the free air; my every phrase a burst of flame; my every chapter a stubborn barricade; my every book a massive stone to crush and flatten the hairy skulls of a people!

There are words as white and fragile and perfumed as jasmine. There are words as sweet and sticky as lolly-pops. There are words as mushy, as warm, as sensuous as the legs of middle-aged adultresses. There are words so celestial, ethereal, exotic, that only the quills of fasting monks of old could scatter them over a sheet of paper like iridescent, tremulous, powdery wings of butterflies. There are words so "public," so commonplace, so lacking in savor, that a prose made up of them falls apart at a touch as stale bread falls into crumbs.

But none of these are the words I choose and prefer. My words must be hard as unbreakable rock: rough, sharp, jagged, cruel as the stones that come down in the landslides, as the breakage from blasts in the quarries. They must be instinctively pagan, shamelessly naked, just as they came from the wine-stained lips of the creative masses. From these rough and homely words I would make a square, solid, substantial, wholesome, and forceful prose, fit to shame the squirters of perfume, the freedmen of the literary literatures. In them I spit out my mucous, get rid of the pus, the gall, the rot in me, vomit up everything upon everybody. And then I too become sweet as the lilies of the valley; delightfully listening in the early morning to the chirping sparrows hopping about on the loose tiles; deliciously weeping as the bells ring in the squatty, crumbling belfries of neglected churches; carefully treading the garden paths outside the city gates, lest my foot fall unwarily on some hard-working ant. And some day you will hear a song rising from my clear heart, so whispering with sighs of bliss, so pregnant with tenderness, so fraught with tears of love, that to hear it will bring back to each of you the warmest, sunniest hour of your youth's passion, but without any wrench of anguish and without the sorrow of a too languid joy.

Chapter 49: Neither Down Nor Out

So they are saying in Italy that I am a man who has run dry, who has sold out his stock, who has reached his limit—a failure! So they say I am a false alarm, a fire of straw—the spring breezes blowing away even the last traces of my ashes?

Not so fast, boys! Just a moment, please! Far from being through I haven't even begun!

You must realize that all I have done—a good deal, you must admit—was just a preface, a prelude, an advance dummy, a flyer, an announcement—if you prefer, froth on the vat of the mash, that boils over to leave the wine clearer underneath. Don't be discouraged. The best is yet to come! I have just been born!

The straw fire was a bonfire! I have given you a Roman candle, a pin-wheel, a fire-cracker, something for you to play with and have a laugh with. But today I feel I can start a conflagration that cannot be put out till the whole world is on fire!

So you have dug my grave! Well, what are you going to put in it—unless perhaps the *corpora delicti* of your own abortions? Anyhow take my advice; chuck the epigraphs you have written for me! The tombstone does not exist that can keep me down. The sentences of death you pronounce upon me give me a

mirth, a hilarity, an energy, a gumption, an impulse
to be up and doing, such as I have not known for a
long, long time.

Listen, gentlemen: I must say it again! Don't mistake silence for a kick at the bucket. Don't mistake
meditation for resignation. Don't mistake study for
suicide. I am thirty, but my hair it still thick, light
and curly. I still have one or two teeth left. I still
have a grip in my hands. I am still shifty on my
feet. I can still feel the blood hammering in my wrists
and temples. There is still a whirl of ideas in my
brain. I can still think, in fact I think better than
ever before. I still have something to say, with time
ahead of me to say it. At home I have pen, ink, and
plenty of paper, smooth white sheets that never stump
my pen. I lack nothing. My hour has not come. You
thought it struck long ago. You were mistaken. Keep
an eye on the clock! I am not surrendering. Neither
do I retreat. Here I am, gentlemen, still on the job;
I, in person, ready to answer all comers on all subjects.

I have so many things to say! You have no idea of
all the impressions I have had, all the discoveries I
have made, things which I must impart to the world
before I die. I cannot condemn, I cannot suppress,
this new part of myself which is the best, the only part
which justifies all the other parts of me.

I owe something to myself, to mankind, to the Spirit.
I feel that I represent in my country and before the
world a trend of ideas that is not well thought of, nor
widely known and understood. I feel that I personify

attack on certain forms of thought and writing which
are disgraceful, pernicious, imbecile. Should I keep
quiet, then, hold my tongue, withdraw to the cell of the
silent observer of men, or into the cozy corner of the
man who plays safe, letting the world go hang so long
as he doesn't miss a meal?

Rather death than such an end! I must get what I
have to say out of my system. I must prevent people
from saying certain things, thinking certain things, and
writing in certain ways. A hopeless task? Never
mind! In all sincerity, I don't care in the least! I
am indifferent to success. Sacrifice! Great and noble
because it is absurd! Sacrifice because it is absurd!
Nothing rational, nothing reasonable was ever called
sacrifice. I feel that I am strong enough to waste my
strength, like a Tantalus, desiring many things I shall
never have. I feel rich enough to throw the best of
my possessions out of the window. Not only have I
not run dry; I can never be pumped dry. The flame
in my soul is the flame which envelops the proud in
the Hell of the Catholics: a flame that will never burn
out. It seems to me as though my youth would be
eternal—like the youth of the Greek gods.

It seems so, I say—but I don't really believe it.
The day will come for me too when the golden scales
will drop from things as the painted linen peels from
powdery mummies. A day will come when the sun
will be naught for me but one more fire in a suffocating
sky; when the return of spring will mean nothing but
the turning of a new page in the almanac; when the

flowers will vainly draw their exquisite colors from the dirty earth to seem more like the sky; when the evening song of the nightingale will be but one of the many sounds of night. And then, when the sun sinks down toward the river I will not climb the steps of the hillsides to bid it farewell with my silent gaze. Blond, sensuous, well-formed women with alluring eyes will go by close to me and my flesh will not be torn with desire (already women are past history with me—I am through with love!). All my life will drift on in languorous indifference, on a dead level, in a fog of gray, even, monotonous memories, with no lightning flashes of desire, no thunderbolts of action. My fate will be everybody's fate!

But before I come to that pass I intend to blow a mighty blast on the trumpets of the universe. I intend to execute all the mandates laid by destiny upon me. I intend to settle all my scores, and leave an enduring record of my words and of my will.

But as yet I have hardly begun. A child is born when he is nine months old, a man when he is thirty. The blossom has come and gone, but the fruit has to ripen before it rots on the tree.

Chapter 50: To the New Generation

WE begin to learn our true market value somewhere
around the age of thirty; for then we are brought up
against men younger than ourselves.

In our teens and in our twenties we have to deal
with the older generation, and that is a fairly simple
proposition. We are judges and hangmen in the name
of an insurgent youth. It too must have a place in the
sun, to open its blossoms. Our enemies have already
arrived: they have won their laurels; and they are
tired—sheepishly hiding their lazy satiety under a
bitter silence and smiles of acrid tolerance. They are
seated on their upholstered thrones and it is too much
work to get up. They look on, they endure us; and
if they are really chicken-hearted, they make advances
to us, and try to hold us off with pretences of welcome.

But now the others begin to come upon the scene,
the youngsters, the fledglings, the first of our posterity,
the boys who were ten and still in school when we were
twenty and just rolling up our sleeves. And this is our
first real test on the scales. These boys have waxed
fat on our ideas. They have dogged our tracks, they
have followed **our** trail, for a good part of the way.
But the time has come for them to change. They are
now of age. They feel that they must now rebel

against those just in front of them. They are preparing to attack us as we attacked our elders.

Even if they do not attack us in public, they discuss us in private. To them we are already history, ripe for appraisal. Already they think they are our superiors. They are sure they have passed us, or can pass us at the first spurt. Between us there no longer prevails the affectionate confidence which bound us to men of our own age, the comradeship that gave us courage in a common competition, and a mutual understanding of our respective shortcomings and weaknesses. These newcomers know it all. They refuse to be told. They belong to another era. They have ripened in other climes. They have other secret passions, other sympathies, other aversions. They step forward coldly brandishing the dogmas of their day, crystallized in phrases of legal tender. They are as cruel as children and as rough as vandals. They belong to another world. They speak a different language. We can be together, work side by side, exchange words and smiles, but we do not understand each other. I feel it, I feel it: there is bad blood between us and them. I feel hanging over my head the sentence of their scorn, their disdainful condemnation.

But listen to me: I have no intention of playing the dead celebrity as so many of our elders did. I shall not pretend to ignore these boys. I shall not hide my head under the pile of my books, or contentedly wrap myself in the toga of a murdered Cæsar. Not in the least! I am I, and they are they! We shall have this scrap out to a finish. I am no more afraid of these youngsters than I was of the old fellows. I am ready to lay my cards on the table, I am ready to defend myself tooth and nail, in words and in ideas. They may choose the weapons. I can fight like a savage, or according to rules. I give no ground. I do not admit that I am beaten. I have already told you: I am neither down nor out. The title of this book is wrong (a matter of small consequence). It tells of a man who sets a high price on his head and who does not intend to throw up the sponge for some time to come.

I do not scorn these children. I do not hate them. Some of them I have helped in every possible way. I did not repel them. I treated them roughly when I thought them worthy of hearing the truth from a grown man. I have watched them, waited for them, been glad to see them, sizing them up as they rounded the corner of their twenties to see what they were good for, what kind of stuff they were made of. I would have been better pleased had they been more violent, more individual, less well behaved, and less like phonographs. But no matter! I respect them, I esteem them, just as they are. If they do many stupid things and write a great deal of nonsense I do not condemn them out of hand. You have to do many worthless things before you are able to do one thing that is passable. No one has a masterpiece ready to pull out of his drawer for his twentieth birthday. I hope they will produce one later on, do things I have not been able to do. I shall feel no jealousy if they go beyond me.

And yet I will not crawl on my stomach before them. I will not leave the ring without fighting till the last gasp. If there is one among them who thinks he can cuff me and walk on me before I am down, he will find that he is dealing with a man with two fists, not with a dough-gut. To destroy they will have to do something themselves. To win they will have to be willing to bleed.

So come on, boys! These thirty years of my life, these twenty years of my study, these ten years of my writing, I might, perhaps, have put to better use. But still I have done something. I have taken part in intellectual movements. I have started some of my own. I have founded reviews. I have published half a dozen books. I have spread my ideas—crazy, stupid, profound, as the case may be—to right and to left. I am somebody. I stand for something. I have a past— and I will have a future at all costs.

And you? What have you done? What are you doing? Let's have a look! Articles, reviews, criticisms—criticisms, reviews, articles! H'm'm! Clever, chaps—I don't deny it. Some ability, I grant you! But so far—if I'm not mistaken—you have been camping on other people's doorsteps, you are still sponging on what others have done. You look like giants because you are standing on piles of other people's books. One or two of you have actually produced some art, or will be producing some! Congratulations! It's hard to judge things,—but still harder to do them. We'll have an eye on you. We'll see! We'll see!

In the meantime I don't intend to be brushed aside, without a quarrel. I will not be trampled on without making a noise. It is for you, for you, more than for any one else, that I have written this dramatization of my mind.

Here I am: I have laid myself open and bare before you; I have exposed my heart and lungs and bowels and nerves to your gaze. I have given you an anatomical mannikin to study. If you care to, you can know me through and through, become acquainted with my most profound, my most real Me. You had better do this. It will save you from many hasty judgments.

These pages are not my biography, but rather an accurate account of my innermost life. The explanation and the key to all the rest of my work are to be found here. This is not a work of art—it is a confession to myself and to others. Here you will learn to know the sentimental and abusive misanthrope for whom, God willing, so many people have felt a profound dislike. I place my soul in your hands. I lay the papers of the prosecution and of the defense before you. On them and by them I prefer to be judged. I will continue to work, to act, with you, at your side. But a part of my life has come to a close, and I insist that you take account of this rambling explosion in fifty chapters.

With all my sorrows, my hopes, and my weaknesses

I offer myself to your cold critical eye. I ask not your pity, not your indulgence, not your praise or consolation, but just three or four hours of your life. If, after you have listened to me, you still believe, in spite of what I have said, that I really am through, that I really am a failure, you will at least have to admit that I failed because I started too many things, that I am nothing because I tried to be everything!

THE END

THE EUROPEAN LIBRARY

THE EUROPEAN LIBRARY

Edited by J. E. SPINGARN

This series is intended to keep Americans in touch with the intellectual and spiritual ferment of the continent of Europe to-day, by means of translations that partake in some measure of the vigor and charm of the originals. No attempt will be made to give what Americans miscall " the best books," if by this is meant conformity to some high and illusory standard of past greatness; any twentieth-century book which displays creative power or a new outlook or more than ordinary interest will be eligible for inclusion. Nor will the attempt be made to select books that merely confirm American standards of taste or morals, since the series is intended to serve as a mirror of European culture and not as a glass through which it may be seen darkly. All forms of literature will be represented, and special attention will be paid to authors whose works have not hitherto been accessible in English.

"The first organized effort to bring into English a series of the really significant figures in contemporary European literature. . . . An undertaking as creditable and as ambitious as any of its kind on the other side of the Atlantic."—*New York Evening Post.*

THE WORLD'S ILLUSION. By JACOB WASSERMANN. Translated by Ludwig Lewisohn. Two volumes.

One of the most remarkable creative works of our time, revolving about the experiences of a man who sums up the wealth and culture of our age yet finds them wanting.

PEOPLE. By PIERRE HAMP. Translated by James Whitall. With Introduction by Elizabeth Shepley Sergeant.

Introducing one of the most significant writers of France, himself a working man, in whom is incarnated the new self-consciousness of the worker's world.

DECADENCE, AND OTHER ESSAYS ON THE CULTURE OF IDEAS. By REMY DE GOURMONT. Translated by William Aspenwall Bradley.

An introduction to Gourmont's theory of the "disassociation of ideas," which has been called "the most fruitful and provocative theory since Nietzsche."

HISTORY: ITS THEORY AND PRACTICE. By BENEDETTO CROCE. Translated by Douglas Ainslie.

A new interpretation of the meaning of history, and a survey of the great historians, by one of the leaders of European thought.

THE NEW SOCIETY. By WALTER RATHENAU. Translated by Arthur Windham.

One of Germany's most influential thinkers and men of action presents his vision of the new society emerging out of the War.

THE REFORM OF EDUCATION. By GIOVANNI GENTILE, Minister of Education in Mussolini's Cabinet. With Introduction by Benedetto Croce. Translated by Dino Bigongiari.

An introduction to the philosophy of a great contemporary thinker who has an extraordinary influence on Italian life to-day.

THE REIGN OF THE EVIL ONE. By C. F. RAMUZ. Translated by James Whitall. With an Introduction by Ernest Boyd.

"A rural fantasia comparable to Synge's 'Playboy,' " introducing an interesting French-Swiss novelist.

THE GOOSE MAN. By JACOB WASSERMANN, author of "The World's Illusion." Translated by Allen W. Porterfield.

A novel which raises the question whether genius can ignore the common rules of humanity without self-destruction.

RUBÉ. By G. A. BORGESE. Translated by Isaac Goldberg.

A novel which has had a sensational success in Italy, centering on the spiritual collapse since the War.

THE PATRIOTEER. By HEINRICH MANN. Translated by Ernest Boyd.

A German "Main Street," describing the career of a typical product of militarism, in school, university, business, and love.

MODERN RUSSIAN POETRY: AN ANTHOLOGY. Translated by Babette Deutsch and A. Yarmolinsky.

Covers the whole field of Russian verse since Pushkin, with the emphasis on contemporary poets.

LIFE OF CHRIST. By GIOVANNI PAPINI. Translated by Dorothy
  Canfield Fisher.
  The first biography of Christ by a great man of letters since Renan's.

THE FAILURE. By GIOVANNI PAPINI. Translated by Virginia Pope.
  An autobiographical novel, serving as a vestibule to the Life of
Christ.

CONTEMPORARY GERMAN POETRY: AN ANTHOLOGY.
  Translated by Babette Deutsch and A. Yarmolinsky.
  Covers the whole field of twentieth century poetry in Germany down
to the latest "expressionists."

TRAVEL DIARIES OF A PHILOSOPHER. By COUNT HERMANN
  KEYSERLING. Translated by J. Holroyd Reece. *In preparation.*
  A philosopher describes life in Asia and America, and broods on
its meaning.

THE CONDUCT OF LIFE. By BENEDETTO CROCE. Translated by
  Arthur Livingston. *In preparation.*
  A volume of searching essays on the moral problems of every-day
life.

SONATAS. By RAMÓN DEL VALLE-INCLÁN. Translated by Thomas
  Walsh. *In preparation.*
  A romance by the most finished artist of modern Spain.

OTHER BOOKS ON FOREIGN LITERATURE BY THE SAME PUBLISHERS

**BENEDETTO CROCE: AN INTRODUCTION TO HIS PHILOSO-
  PHY.** By RAFFAELLO PICCOLI.
  The first adequate account of Croce's life and thought.

A GUIDE TO RUSSIAN LITERATURE. By M. J. OLGIN.
  A popular handbook describing the life and works of some sixty
Russian authors.

HARCOURT, BRACE AND COMPANY
Publishers   New York